GOD made the WORLD & ME

Thirteen Comprehensive 6-in-1 Curriculum Lessons

Includes Special Centers for
Older Students & Younger Students

written by
Susan Laurita

with
Helen Haidle
& David Haidle

Master
Books®
A Division of New Leaf Publishing Group
www.masterbooks.com

MasterBooks® CURRICULUM

Author: David & Helen Haidle,
Susan Laurita

Master Books Creative Team:

Editor: Laura Welch

Design: David Haidle

Cover Design: Diana Bogardus

Cover Illustrations: David Haidle

Copy Editors:

Judy Lewis

Willow Meek

Curriculum Review:

Kristen Pratt

Laura Welch

Diana Bogardus

God Made the World and Me
Thirteen 6-in-1 Comprehensive Curriculum Lessons

First printing: April 2009
Second printing: August 2020

ISBN-13: 978-0-89051-563-1
Library of Congress Control Number: 2009923583

Printed in the United States of America

Please visit our Web site for other great titles:
www.masterbooks.com

All Scripture is from the King James Version of the Bible,
unless otherwise noted.

Photo Credits
All images are Shutterstock unless otherwise noted.
clipart.com: 35, 43, 44, 119, 127, 139, 150, 151

David and Helen Haidle own Seed Faith Books in Portland, OR and their books have been bestsellers in the Christian market and won several industry awards. Over the years this talented couple has written and illustrated unique books for students, churches, and ministries. They have also taught a variety of workshops at Oregon Christian Writers conferences and at homeschool conferences.

GOD made the WORLD & ME

written by
Susan Laurita

with

Helen Haidle
& David Haidle

Master
Books®
A Division of New Leaf Publishing Group
www.masterbooks.com

GOD made the WORLD & ME
for Preschoolers

Summary of Introductory Pages
for Leaders & Teachers

Scope & Sequence Lesson Outline
Six Science, Physical, & Art Learning Centers

Circle Time Songs

The "Creation Song" by Susan Laurita

Sing to the tune of "Frere Jacques" ("Are You Sleeping, Brother John?").

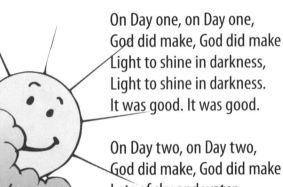

On Day one, on Day one,
God did make, God did make
Light to shine in darkness,
Light to shine in darkness.
It was good. It was good.

On Day two, on Day two,
God did make, God did make
Lots of sky and water,
Lots of sky and water.
It was good. It was good.

On Day three, on Day three,
God did make, God did make
Many trees and flowers,
Many trees and flowers.
It was good. It was good.

On Day four, on Day four,
God did make, God did make
Sun and moon and stars,
Sun and moon and stars.
It was good. It was good.

On Day five, on Day five,
God did make, God did make
All the fish and birdies,
All the fish and birdies.
It was good. It was good.

On Day six, on Day six,
God did make, God did make
All the other animals,
All the other animals.
God made man, woman too.

(more slowly)
On Day seven, on Day seven,
God did rest, God did rest.
All the work was finished,
All the work was finished.
It was good, very good!

More Songs:

"Everything Is Possible"
Everything is possible with our God.
Everything is possible with our God.
Stand up where you are and give a little nod.
Everything is possible with our God.
With our God, with our God,
Stand up where you are and give a little nod.
Everything is possible with our God.

"He's Got the Whole World in His Hands"
"Head and Shoulders, Knees and Toes"
"Jesus Loves the Little Children"
"My God Is So Big"
"Jesus Loves Me"
"God Is So Good"
"God Made Me"

Introduction for Parents and Teachers

Dear Parents and Teachers,

God Made the World and Me is a hands-on curriculum designed to ignite, or reignite, the child's wonder at the world around them. Research shows that children (and adults) who are more exposed to nature benefit physically, emotionally, and spiritually.

The preschool-years are the perfect time to introduce science in a way that involves the child and engages his/her imagination and senses. Preschool-age children are in awe of the world around them, and desire to know how everything works. What better way to start than by introducing God who created the whole universe and everything in it . . . including them? **Science, Physical, and Art Learning Centers** will provide unique learning experiences and activities for each lesson. **Circle Time** can include *The Creation Story for Children* book, and will teach children a Bible Memory Verse plus another verse of our "Creation Song."

Take-home Parent Pages share information about what happens in the classroom. These notes contain suggestions to help prepare children for a successful experience. There is usually something related to the lesson for a child to bring to class each week. Parents, please do your best to send the items indicated when needed. Your child will love bringing something to use in class, and so will your child's teacher.

The **hands-on activities** in these lessons are geared to invite participation, soothe emotions, encourage independence and creativity, and remind children that God is big, capable, personal, and loving. **The activities** may be considered more "messy" than traditional lessons. Be forewarned, but not discouraged. As a teacher of preschoolers, I have tried these activities in my own class and I know from experience they can be done. More than that, I know the investment in our children is well worth it.

May God bless each of you and your children, as you explore God's creation together.

Joyfully,
Susan Laurita, Author, *God Made the World and Me*

Note: *Creation Big Book* is no longer available.

Introduction for Leaders

Each lesson uses a Scripture Verse that corresponds with an illustration from *The Creation Story for Children* book.

"In the beginning, God created the heaven and the earth" (Genesis 1:1 NKJV).

The KJV (King James Version) is used.
(Note: Feel free to substitute any other version of Scripture you prefer.)

NOTE: This section provides a checklist to prepare for each lesson.

Get Ready:
☐ **PRAY**
☐ **MAKE COPIES**
☐ **CONTACT ASSISTANTS**
☐ **PREPARE**
☐ **GATHER**

God Creates . . .

6 Learning Centers
To involve children before and after Circle Time Learning
Physical Center, Science Center, Art Center, Older/Younger Students

David & Helen Haidle

Helen and David have written and illustrated 45 books during the past 20 years. Their award-winning books have won three C. S. Lewis Awards and three CBA Silver Medallions. With sales of over 1,700,000, the Haidles' books help families, churches, and schools present God's love to children. Their recent publications provide resources on Psalm 23 and Creation. The Haidles' new non-profit organization, HEART GIFTS, provides thousands of books to needy children.

Suggested Teaching Schedules

The lessons in this books are adaptable for all children's programs. They can last for as little as one week or as long as three months. Suggested time frames are listed below. Use the parts of the lessons best suited for your children and program resources.

Christian Schools or Church Sunday School/Sabbath School/Mid-Week Services:
Thirteen Lessons — One lesson a week for a quarter (three months)

Homeschool Study: Three months (13 weeks) on CREATION
Can study one lesson per week for 13 weeks
(Focus on one learning center four days each week)

Preschool/Child Care: One Lesson each week for 13 weeks
or spend one month (four weeks) on CREATION
Week 1   Lessons 1–3
Week 2   Lessons 4–6
Week 3   Lessons 7–9
Week 4   Lessons 10–13

Vacation Bible School: Usually meets for only a week
Monday   Lessons 1– 4
Tuesday   Lessons 5– 6
Wednesday   Lessons 7– 8
Thursday   Lessons 9–10
Friday   Lessons 11–13

Susan Laurita, Author

Susan Laurita is the Director of Professional Early Education Resources (PEERS), a division of PROEEA. Susan has a BA in Early Childhood Education, an MS in Family Support, and over 30 years in the field. Her driving passion is to encourage in children, staff, and families a lifelong love of learning. Her strengths include teacher training, writing, parent education, curriculum development, and accreditation.

Note for Leaders of Preschool Groups

The week or session BEFORE you begin this CREATION series of lessons with your preschoolers, copy and send home this special **PARENT PAGE** found on the next page of this introduction section.

This information, along with several suggestions for activities to be done at home, will help parents prepare their child for a positive experience of learning when they come to your next class.

One important thing about this curriculum is that it invites children and parents in and makes use of all of their senses. But if you do not have time or resources to set up ALL the learning centers and everything that is listed, don't worry. Do the best you can with your time and resources.

Ask God to use your time and talents to encourage in children a love for learning and an awe for the Lord of Creation. Let God's Holy Spirit do the rest! Our blessings to you as you invest in children and families for eternity.

—Susan Laurita, author

Note on RESOURCES: Oriental Trading Company, Inc., sells many items that can be used for room decorations and for the six Learning Centers each week.

Plastic magnifying glasses, bubbles, bottles, Break-Your-Own-Geode rocks, smiling sun and hanging stars, palm tree and flower decorations, seashells, sand dollars, starfish, sea life decoration assortment, foam parrots, animal puppets, and/or bean bags *(Fin, Feathers, Fur game)*, plus dolphin balloons and flower leis for the Creation Celebration (#13).

Dear Parents,

Next Time: we begin a series on CREATION. Each session will have a science learning center, a physical learning center, and an art learning center related to one specific day of creation. After each lesson, your child will bring home a note explaining what we have done in class, and how you can help your child prepare for next class session.

This Time: Help your child focus on the concepts of "empty" and "light and darkness."

Suggestions:

1. Schedule an "empty event" when you hand your children "empty" containers for them to fill themselves. *(Examples: dishes at meal times, snack plates, crayon boxes, bathtubs, etc.)* Then switch roles. Let your children hand you "empty" things.

2. Make a list of things your child does in the light. Make a second list of the things your child does at night. Compare the two lists. Ask your child which he/she prefers.

Read Genesis 1:1–5 to your child this week. Pray for your child and for his/her teachers.

Things to Bring to the NEXT class: a flashlight marked with your child's name on it.

God's blessings to your family from your Teaching Staff.

copy and distribute

Dear Parents,

Lesson 1

Next Time: we begin a series on CREATION. Each session will have a science learning center, a physical learning center, and an art learning center related to one specific day of creation. After each lesson, your child will bring home a note explaining what we have done in class, and how you can help your child prepare for next class session.

This Time: Help your child focus on the concepts of "empty" and "light and darkness."

Suggestions:

1. Schedule an "empty event" when you hand your children "empty" containers for them to fill themselves. *(Examples: dishes at meal times, snack plates, crayon boxes, bathtubs, etc.)* Then switch roles. Let your children hand you "empty" things.

2. Make a list of things your child does in the light. Make a second list of the things your child does at night. Compare the two lists. Ask your child which he/she prefers.

Read Genesis 1:1–5 to your child this week. Pray for your child and for his/her teachers.

Things to Bring to the NEXT class: a flashlight marked with your child's name on it.

God's blessings to your family from your Teaching Staff.

God Creates LIGHT

"In the beginning, God created the heaven and the earth. . . And God said, 'Let there be light.' And there was light. And God saw the light, that it was good: and God divided the light from the darkness. God called the light Day, and the darkness he called Night. And the evening and the morning were the first day" (Genesis 1:1, 3-5 KJV).

Get Ready:

☐ **PRAY** throughout the week that God will bless you and your children with understanding of the awesome power of His creation.

☐ **MAKE COPIES** of the parent take-home page (for a group class).

☐ **CONTACT ASSISTANTS** and go over the things you would like them to do in class.

☐ **PREPARE** and set up your teaching areas to be used for the learning centers and Circle Time activities.

☐ **GATHER** *The Creation Story for Children* (optional) plus supplies and materials for your centers and circle time.

Welcome parents and children as they arrive.
Remember to call each one by name.
Invite children to join one of the learning centers

Learning Center Supplies

Physical Center
flashlights
Science Center
#1 – flashlight and a prism
#2 – tub of water, cornstarch, towels for cleanup
Art Center
half sheets of black or dark-blue construction paper, drinking straws for each student, white tempera paint, and silver glitter (optional)
Older/Younger Students
• flashlight, cardstock, books, scissors, a table.
• half sheets of black or dark-blue construction paper, white tempera or finger paint, white pencil or chalk, spoon to scoop paint, paint smocks, water, towels

Learning Centers

(To involve children before and after Circle Time Learning)

Physical Center

Flashlight Tag

Supplies Needed: flashlights, chairs (Hopefully some of the children brought flashlights from home.)

Choose one child to be "it." Let him use his own flashlight or loan him yours.

Explain:

1. When it's your turn to be "it," you will try to catch one of your friends.

2. You can "tag" any person by shining your light on the other person's body.

3. So if someone shines the light on your body, you are "caught" or "captured."

Then you must go and sit down on the floor with other children who have been captured by the person who is "it."
You can't get up and run away, but you can cheer for those who are being chased.

4. When all of the children have been caught, then another child will have a turn to be "it," and we can start the tag game all over again.

Science Center

Option #1

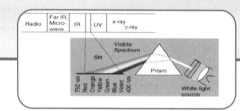

Supplies Needed: a flashlight and a prism (optional: a color wheel)

Let children tell what they already know.

*   Guess what will happen when you turn on the flashlight. *(Light will shine out.)*

*   What color is the light? *(White/yellowish)* Are there any other colors in light? *(No.)*

*   What about the prism?
    Have you ever seen a prism?
    What color is the prism?
    Let's shine the light through a prism and find out what colors we will see.

(Now shine a light through the prism to get a very clear rainbow of colors. Show the color wheel.)

*   Look at all the colors! What colors do you see? Where did the colors come from?
    When God gave us light, God also gave us all the colors we enjoy every day.
    ALL the colors are part of all the "light." We just can't see the colors until the prism breaks them apart into a rainbow.

*   Now let's all tell our favorite color.
    (Let children take turns holding the flashlight and prism as they tell their favorite color.)

Learning Centers

Science Center

Option #2

Supplies Needed: tub of water, cornstarch, towels for cleanup

• Let children feel the cornstarch before you add it to the water.

• Once cornstarch is added to water, let children take turns trying to pull some of the cornstarch out of the tub.

Explain: The cornstarch feels somewhat solid before we put it into the tub of water, but when it's wet it slips through your fingers. That is called "formless" because it has no shape at all.

Discuss:

1. Does this mixture have a special "shape"? *(No. Nothing at all.)*

2. What if WE were like this? *(We wouldn't have any form without bones and skin holding our bodies together.)*

3. What if the whole world was like this tub of water and cornstarch? The world used to be like this. It was formless before God made everything.

4. Do you like the world the way it is now with all the plants, animals, and our bodies? YES! Let's thank God that we have a shape and a form.

Older Children

Supplies Needed: flashlight, cardstock, books, scissors, and a table

1. On the center of the table, prop the piece of cardstock up with books on either side.

2. Put the flashlight at the end of the table pointing in the direction of the cardstock.
    • Where will the light go when I turn on the flashlight?
    • Will it hit the paper, or will it end up somewhere else?

3. Check your answers by turning on a flashlight.

4. Now draw a circle around the light on the cardstock. Cut out the circle. Replace the cardstock in its standing up position.
    • Now where will the light go? Test it. The light goes straight to the wall.

5. Explain: Light travels in a straight line. That makes it easy to remember God made it on Day 1. *(Hold up your index finger. Have children hold up one finger also.)*

Learning Centers

Art Center

Supplies Needed: half sheets of black or dark-blue construction paper, drinking straws for each student, white tempera paint, silver glitter (optional)

NOTE: If you do this art project as a large group activity, have the children clean up their area when they finish their painting. Have them join one of the other centers.

If not done as a group activity, you also could read some books about night and day.

NOTE: Finger paint recipe on final page of this lesson. Use heavy paper.

1. On a half sheet of black or dark-blue construction paper, drop a tablespoon size of white paint.

2. Have the children blow GENTLY through a drinking straw at the paint.
   This will help spread the paint in all directions and create a nice "burst of light."
   Can let the children sprinkle small amounts of glitter on their splattered paintings.

3. Put names on papers and allow to dry.

Younger Children

Supplies Needed: half sheets of black or dark—blue construction paper, white tempera or finger paint, white pencil or chalk (to write their names), teaspoon for putting paint on paper, paint smocks, water and towels (for washing up)

This is very similar to the ART activity for the older children.
EXCEPTION: do *not* ask these youngest children to blow through a straw.

Instead, show them how to make splashes of LIGHT by using their fingers or their whole hands to spread the paint around the paper.

As they work, talk about how God made light shine into the dark. Now we don't have to live in darkness. We thank God for making light shine in our world. The light helps us remember how much God loves us.

NOTE: Be ready to help children wash up when they finish.

Invite children to come to Circle Time to join you.

Circle Time Song

Introduce the "Creation Song."
Sing to the tune of "Frere Jacques" ("Are You Sleeping?").

On Day one, on Day one,

God did make, God did make

Light to shine in darkness,

Light to shine in darkness.

It was good. It was good.

Other Songs:

"This Little Light of Mine" and "All Night, All Day"

Ask the children for other favorites.

* * * * *

GAME: **Night and Day**

Ask children to name routine activities they do on a regular basis. *(brush teeth, lay on a pillow, put on some shoes, eat dinner, drink a glass of water, play with toys, help mother, cover up with a blanket, comb your hair, shut your eyes, go to the store, take a bath)*

Explain:

*   When I name something you do in the DAY, then you should frame your face with your hands, and smile at me.

*   When I name something you do at NIGHT, then you should cover your eyes with your hands.

Circle Time Discussion

NOTE: Bring flashlights to Circle Time.

"In the beginning, God created the heaven and the Earth" (Genesis 1:1).

Discuss:
At first, the earth was dark and empty. What was the world like when it was empty? Do you think God was there?
What about other things we can't see?
Was music in the world?
Were colors in the world?
Was love in the world? *(Yes! God is love.)*
(All answers are acceptable).

Let's see if we can make our room look like the Earth at the beginning.
(Turn out lights. Close blinds. Turn off music. Have the children sit down, close their eyes, and listen to no sound at all.)

Raise your hand if you like the world this way. Now open your eyes. We know that God didn't leave the world this way. What do you think God did first?
(Take all answers.)

Optional: Find out what God did as we read pages 3–4 of the *The Creation Story for Children* book.

Who guessed right about what God made first? *(Light)*

Read both pages again, but this time when you say "Let there be light" ask everyone to turn on their flashlights and shine them at the ceiling as they join you in saying,

"Let there be light!"

See what a difference LIGHT makes!
Do you like it better in darkness or in light? Why?
What did God say about the light?
(It was good.)

Can we turn darkness into light without our flashlights or classroom lights? *(No! Only God can make light.)*

What kinds of things can you do in the daylight that you cannot do at night?
(Take all answers.)

The Bible tells us, *"God is light. There is no darkness in him at all"* (1 John 1:5).

Aren't we glad that GOD IS LIGHT and that God made light on Day 1? Next time we will find out what God made on Day 2.

Now let's practice our Bible Memory Verse.

Practice the Memory Verse

"God said, 'Let there be light,' and there was light" (Genesis 1:3 KJV).

• Sit together with child(ren) in a circle with all of your flashlights pointed up.

• Repeat the memory verse together several times.

• Turn on all your flashlights when you say:

God said, **"Let there be light!"**

Post-Session Learning Centers

(After Circle Time, rotate children to another Learning Center)

Closing • Back to Circle Time

At the end of the class, gather the children together for a closing circle.
(Hold Bible as you read the first verse:)

Listen carefully as I read you the first verse of the Bible.
"In the beginning God made the heaven and the earth."

Now all of you say the verse with me. *(In the beginning . . . God made . . . the heaven . . . and the earth.)*
What was the world like in the beginning? *(Dark, no plants or animals, etc.)*
What did God make on Day 1? *(Light — God said, "Let there be light.")*

Have the children tell what their favorite part of the day was.
Help them review each step. Then pray together.
Thank You, God, for loving us. Thank You for making the heavens and the Earth. We are glad You created so much LIGHT for us to enjoy. Amen.

Remember to send home Parent Page

Dear Parents,

Today: We talked about God making light in a dark world. We played flashlight tag, saw light break into colors by shining light through a prism, and the older children even learned that light travels in a straight line, which helps us remember God made light on Day 1.
Ask your child to sing the first verse of the Creation Song.

Next Time: We will talk about God creating SKY. The sky looks different every day, depending on the weather. Why not take this week to make a graph of how the sky looks each day. Discuss with your child why the sky looks different, or the same. Which kind of sky did you see the most during the week? Which kind of sky does your child like best? Why do you think God gave us different kinds of weather? How does weather affect us?

Read: Genesis 1:6—8 with your child. Pray with your child for his/her teachers and class.

Bring Next Time: Your homemade graph of the different kinds of skies.

For Parents: Watching the sky reminds all of us that no matter what the weather is, God's love is never-changing, constant, and entirely reliable. God's love for us never ends nor wavers.

Blessings to your family from our Teaching Staff

copy and distribute

Dear Parents,

Lesson 1

Today: We talked about God making light in a dark world. We played flashlight tag, saw light break into colors by shining light through a prism, and the older children even learned that light travels in a straight line, which helps us remember God made light on Day 1.
Ask your child to sing the first verse of the Creation Song.

Next Time: We will talk about God creating SKY. The sky looks different every day, depending on the weather. Why not take this week to make a graph of how the sky looks each day? Discuss with your child why the sky looks different, or the same. Which kind of sky did you see the most during the week? Which kind of sky does your child like best? Why do you think God gave us different kinds of weather? How does weather affect us?

Read: Genesis 1:6—8 with your child. Pray with your child for his/her teachers and class.

Bring Next Time: Your homemade graph of the different kinds of skies.

For Parents: Watching the sky reminds all of us that no matter what the weather is, God's love is never-changing, constant, and entirely reliable. God's love for us never ends nor wavers.

Blessings to your family from our Teaching Staff

God Creates LIGHT

"In the beginning, God created the heaven and the earth…
And God said, 'Let there be light.' And there was light.
And God saw the light, that it was good" (Genesis 1:1, 3-5 KJV).

Magazine COLOR Collage

Supplies Needed: assortment of magazines, scissors, glue sticks, 11"x17" white paper

1. Hand out magazines to the children. Make sure everyone has at least one magazine.

Kindergartners will enjoy the hunt for images. They will also benefit from some simple guidelines and from taking time to use a scissors.

2. Hand out white paper, scissors, and a glue stick.

3. Explain how LIGHT is made up of all the colors of the rainbow. Have each child choose one color, then collect different objects or swatches of that color from the magazines.

4. Have children glue their cut-out images onto their piece of paper. Encourage students to overlap images and fill up as much of the paper as they can.

NOTE: This is really simple, but the fact that each picture has a color theme unifies the images and can create some stunning artwork. Plus, everyone is getting lots of scissors cutting practice, without really thinking about it!

Easy Fingerpaint
for Art Activity Center

Supplies Needed:

2 cups white flour
2 cups cold water
food coloring

Directions:

Put water into a large bowl. Slowly add the flour, while the children are stirring. Once it's all mixed together, divide into smaller bowls and add food coloring.

God Creates the SKY

God said, "Let there be a firmament in the midst of the waters, and let it divide the waters (above) from the waters (below). God called the firmament Heaven. And the evening and the morning were the second day" (Genesis 1:6–8 KJV).

Welcome parents and children as they arrive.
Remember to call each one by name.
Invite children to join one of the learning centers.

Get Ready:

☐ PRAY throughout the week that God will bless you and your children with understanding of the awesome power of His creation.

☐ MAKE COPIES of the parent take-home page. (for a group class)

☐ CONTACT ASSISTANTS
Go over the things you would like them to do in class.

☐ PREPARE a large graph or chart to record the different kinds of sky each day this week.
(Record sunrise, morning, noon, evening, sunset, night.)

☐ GATHER *The Creation Story for Children* (optional) plus other materials for your centers and circle time.

Learning Center Supplies

Physical Center
None

Science Center
your graph of the different kinds of sky, a marker, books and/or pictures about weather or various skies

Art Center
#1 – half sheets of light-blue construction paper, cotton balls, glue sticks, pictures of various skies
#2 – construction paper, crayons or markers, music with "weather sounds"

Older/Younger Students
• clear glass jar with a lid, cup of hot water, warming tray, *Creation Big Book* (Optional: aluminum pie pan filled with ice cubes)

• half sheets of light-blue construction paper, cotton balls, glue sticks, pictures of various skies

Learning Centers
(To involve children before and after Circle Time Learning)

Physical Center

Supplies Needed: none

Ask the children to join you in a circle.

- Now we will play a game about the different kinds of sky and the different kinds of weather God made.

- When I say a certain kind of weather, then you should pretend like you are outside in that kind of weather.

Now let's practice together:
Sunny: put out "beach towel" and lie down

Rainy: put up a pretend umbrella

Snowy: pretend to throw snowballs

Windy: walk backward two steps, wave arms to keep from falling over

After the children have tried each action, start the game. Begin slowly.
Then call the words out faster and faster.
Finally, slow down until your time is up.

(Note: It is important to end slowly, otherwise children won't settle down to listen at Circle Time.)

Thank You, God, for the sky and the weather.

Science Center

Supplies Needed: your graph of the different kinds of sky, a marker

Have the children show their graphs from home when they recorded the weather.

Discuss:
- What did you find out about the sky this week?
- How many sunny days did you find?
- How many rainy days? Snowy days? Cloudy days? Windy days?
- Does the sky look the same all day long? Why not?
- Who made the sky? Would it be hard to make a big sky above the earth? God put lots of weather into the sky.

Today we will find out what kind of skies you like the best during the day.

Have each child come up and put an "X" in the row next to his/her favorite kind of sky.

Remember to include yourself and your assistants at the end. Count them up and announce the classroom results.

Learning Centers

Art Center

Option #1

NOTE: The art project can be done as a large—group activity or as a Learning Center.

Supplies Needed: half—sheets of light blue construction paper, cotton balls, glue sticks, several pictures of blue sky to show children examples of various skies

God made our big sky. Now we will make pictures of a blue sky with fluffy clouds in it. You can make the clouds any way you want.

If you pull the cotton ball apart slowly, your clouds will look smooth and wispy. If you pull the cotton ball out just a little, your clouds will look fluffier. Or you can make your clouds look like a picture of something else.

1. Decide how you want your clouds to look.
2. Glue the cotton balls on your paper to make a sky.

Another Option:
- Use colored chalk on dark blue paper to illustrate God's creation on Day 2.
- Give each child a cotton ball attached to a clothespin. Dip cotton in white tempera paint.
- Swish cotton ball with white tempera paint over the chalk to make clouds. *Voila!* Everyone will have a special "sky picture" *(Pam Crane, Everson, WA).*

Older Children

Supplies Needed: glass jar with a lid, a cup of boiling water, and a warming tray (Optional: aluminum pie pan with ice cubes)

1. Pour hot water into the jar.
2. Put the lid on tight *(or place an aluminum pie pan full of ice cubes on top of jar opening).*
3. Place jar on the warming tray.

Explain: The Bible tells us God separated the water "below" from the water "above" the earth. How does the water "below" go up into the sky? Let's see how that happens.

4. Watch as condensation makes the water form droplets on the side of the jar *(and also on the bottom of the aluminum pie pan if that is used).*

Explain: This is called evaporation. It is how clouds are formed. First the drops form together and make a big cloud. When the drops get heavy enough, the drops fall back down. That's when it rains on the Earth.

Learning Centers

Art Center

Option #2

*Supplies Needed: construction paper, crayons or markers,
music that includes "weather sounds" (thunder, storm, rain, etc.)*

Explain: Today I brought some music with lots of "weather sounds" in it.

1. God made our sky with lots of weather. Let's listen to this music.
2. You tell me what weather sounds you hear in the music.
3. Now let's draw a picture of what it would be like to be inside the music.

- If you hear rain, be sure to put rain in your picture.
- If you hear sunshine, put in lots of bright light.
- What will you include if you think you hear snow?
- What about thunder and lightning? Anything is okay. It is your picture.

NOTE: If you do the art project as a large group activity, ask the children to clean up their areas when they are finished, then join one of the other centers.

Younger Children

NOTE: Art Center — Option #1 will work well with younger children. The difference will be in the finished product.

Supplies Needed: half sheets of light blue construction paper, cotton balls, glue sticks, pictures of blue sky to show children examples of various skies

1. You may want to pull the cotton balls apart for the children. Hand out the cotton balls a few at a time.

2. You may also ask some of the younger children who aren't normally interested in art to just pull the "clouds" apart for others to use. This will help the youngest children develop fine–motor control.

**Invite children to come to
Circle Time to join you.**

Circle Time Song

Review the first verse of the "Creation Song."
Teach the second verse.
Sing to the tune of "Frere Jacques" ("Are You Sleeping?").

On Day one, on Day one,
God did make, God did make
Light to shine in darkness,
Light to shine in darkness.
It was good. It was good.

On Day two, on Day two,
God did make, God did make
Lots of sky and water,
Lots of sky and water.

It was good. It was good.

*   *   *

Other Songs:

"Everything Is Possible"

"Good Morning, Clouds"
*(Song found in "Tunes for Tots" by Warner
and Berry, the Lollipop Learning Series.)*

Circle Time Discussion

Discuss:
Look at the picture. What do you see?
(Sky, clouds, water).

Next week we will talk about the water. Can you see the water going up into the sky? The clouds are filling up with water. Soon rain will fall from the clouds.

Today let's look at the sky.
Is there enough sky for everyone on earth to enjoy? Yes. Sky covers the earth. Everyone can see the sky.

Do you think the sky looks the same from everywhere on earth?
When have you seen the sky look different? *(Times of storm, sunset, clear sky, sunrise, cloudy, etc.)*

Have any of you ever been up in the sky?
(Airplane, balloon ride, etc.)
What was it like to be high in the sky?

What does it make you feel like when you go up in a plane and see the clouds?

What is your favorite thing about the sky God made? *(Color of it, clouds, etc.)*

How big is the sky God made?
Have you looked up in the sky at night?
Some people look through telescopes at the sky.
How high does the sky go?
(The Bible says it is huge! Telescopes can't see far enough to find an "end" of the sky.)

Can we make something as big as the sky?
(No! Only God can!)

If we all stood together and stretched out our arms, could we make something as big as the sky? Let's try.

(After the children have stood up, stretched out their arms and tried, have them sit in a circle around you.)

We may not be able to make something as big as the sky, but I know each one of us can learn a verse that tells us about the sky.

Now let's practice our
Bible Memory Verse.

Practice the Memory Verse

"God called the firmament Heaven" (Genesis 1:8 KJV).
(paraphrase: God called the big space 'sky.')

Now let's practice this verse as if we were a class of popping corn.

Have each child in turn, pop up and say the next word in the verse.

God . . . called . . . the . . . firmament . . . Heaven (Genesis 1:8).

God . . . called . . . the . . . big . . . space . . . sky (Genesis 1:8).

Continue around the circle until the words come easily for everyone.

Post-Session Learning Centers

(After Circle Time, rotate children to another Learning Center)

Closing • Back to Circle Time

At the end of the class, gather the children together for a closing circle. Have the children tell what their favorite part of the day was. Help them review each step.

Then pray together.
Thank You, God, for making the sky and all of the different kinds of weather for us to enjoy. Thank You for making a sky so big that everyone on earth can enjoy it at the same time. We thank You for this wonderful world. In Jesus' Name we pray. Amen.

Does anyone remember what I said we will talk about next time?
(Water)

Remember to send home Parent Page

Dear Parents,

Today: We found out God made the sky. We graphed our favorite sky and made sky pictures. We played a game about different kinds of weather. We talked about how God made the sky SO big we can all enjoy it at once. Older children did an experiment to see how God makes rain. Ask your child to sing the first two verses of the Creation Song. Ask what they liked best today.

Next Time: We will talk about God making water. Water is a very important part of all creation. To prepare, make a list with your child of everything you do with water on one day. Keep the list handy. As you come to new things, simply add it to the list.

Read Genesis 1:6–8 again with your child. Pray with your child for his/her class and thank God for the great gift of water.

Bring next time: Your list of water activities plus clothes you don't mind getting wet!

For Parents: God wants YOU to be like a well-watered garden, like a spring of water that never runs dry. Look to the Lord to renew your joy and faith (Isa. 58:11).

Blessings to your family from our Teaching Staff

copy and distribute

Dear Parents,

Lesson 2

Today: We found out God made the sky. We graphed our favorite sky and made sky pictures. We played a game about different kinds of weather. We talked about how God made the sky SO big we can all enjoy it at once. Older children did an experiment to see how God makes rain. Ask your child to sing the first two verses of the Creation Song. Ask what they liked best today.

Next Time: We will talk about God making water. Water is a very important part of all creation. To prepare, make a list with your child of everything you do with water on one day. Keep the list handy. As you come to new things, simply add it to the list.

Read Genesis 1:6–8 again with your child. Pray with your child for his/her class and thank God for the great gift of water.

Bring next time: Your list of water activities plus clothes you don't mind getting wet!

For Parents: God wants YOU to be like a well-watered garden, like a spring of water that never runs dry. Look to the Lord to renew your joy and faith (Isa. 58:11).

Blessings to your family from our Teaching Staff

God said, "Let there be a firmament in the midst of the waters, and let it divide the waters (above) from the waters (below) (Genesis 1:6–8 KJV).

A Sky Full of AIR

Supplies Needed: a balloon

Blow up a balloon in front of the hildren.
Hold up the balloon and ask the children:

WHAT is inside the balloon? *(Air)*

How do you know there is air in the balloon? *(Saw you blow in it)*
See the shape of the balloon. When I push on it, you know
air is inside by how the balloon changes shape. *(Demonstrate)*

Watch what happens when I release the air. *(Slowly release air
from the opening so it blows your hair or something that will move.)*

Even though we can't see the air, we can see what the air does.
When have you seen something moved by the air? *(When wind blows, we see
evidence of the air as it moves clouds, leaves, grass, flowers, etc.)*

How many of you have felt the air blow on your skin?
Why else do we need air? *(So we and other living creatures can breathe.)*

Are you glad God loves us so much that He made a big sky full of AIR so we could
breathe? Yes, THANK YOU, GOD, for air.

Finger Play — RAIN

Rain falls on the grass; *(flutter fingers along with ground)*

Rain falls on the tree; *(Stand up straight, stretch arms like branches)*

Rain falls on the housetop, *(Touch finger tips, use hands to form roof top)*

But not on me! *(Point to self and shake head "no")*

God Creates WATER

God said, "Let the water under the heaven be gathered together unto one place and let the dry land appear: and it was so. And God called the dry land Earth; and the gathering together of the waters called he Seas. And God saw that it was good" (Genesis 1:9–10 KJV).

Get Ready:

☐ **PRAY** throughout the week that God will bless you and your children with understanding of the awesome power of His creation.

☐ **MAKE COPIES** of the parent take-home page (for a group class).

☐ **CONTACT ASSISTANTS** Go over the things you would like them to do in class.

☐ **PREPARE** 10–12 file cards with words written on them describing ways you use water.

Examples: swimming, drinking, cooking food, bathing, washing clothes, cleaning floors, washing the car, etc. Also make a large graph with the children's names written down one side.

☐ **GATHER** *The Creation Story for Children* (optional) plus a globe or map for your circle time.

Welcome parents and children as they arrive.
Remember to call each one by name.
Invite children to join one of the learning centers.

Learning Center Supplies

Physical Center
#1 – bubble solution, upbeat music
#2 – use furniture in room for obstacle course

Science Center
plastic tub to hold water, a variety of containers that will NOT float, some "sink and float" items, towels for cleanup, a large pitcher (or two) of water

Art Center
construction paper, crayons, paintbrushes, blue wash (diluted blue tempera paint), plastic tablecloth

Older/Younger Students
• your file cards with words listing the ways you use water, your graph with the children's names, markers, a glass jar filled with tap water, plus a bottle of fresh water
• use the Science Center and its supplies or set up a separate water table with plastic containers

Learning Centers

(To involve children before and after Circle Time Learning)

Physical Center

Option #1

Supplies Needed: Bible, bubble solution, upbeat music (Open Bible to Genesis 1.) Can use cotton string.

Remember the very first verse in the Bible? *"In the beginning God made the heaven and the earth"* (Genesis 1:1).

Let's say it together. *(Repeat verse.)*

I'm glad God created the heaven and the Earth, aren't you?

God also created sky and water. I'm glad we have lots of water! Now watch me blow bubbles with this soapy water.

I will blow a bunch of bubbles up in the air and you see if you can catch them.

Oh, where will all these bubbles land?

(Turn on music. Let the children move creatively while you blow bubbles over and around them.)

Discuss: Can we make bubbles without any water? *(No.)* God knows we can have a lot of fun with water. Tell me some of your favorite things to do with water or in water. *(Splash in rain puddles, swim in lakes and pools, play in bathtub, paint with watercolors, make lemonade to drink, wash a doll, etc.)*

Physical Center

Option #2

Supplies Needed: a variety of furniture in the classroom

1. Who remembers how LIGHT travels?
    Does it go in a straight line or around corners? *(Straight line.)*

2. Today we will make an "obstacle course" to show how *water* travels.
    This obstacle course will be full of blocks that force the water away as it moves.
    Help me make an obstacle course on this end of the room.
    Let's use the furniture to make block the water as it flows through the room.

3. Then watch how we will go through the course, weaving in and out and around the obstacles. This is a good way to find out how water travels.
    Now let's each take a turn. Does water travel in a straight line like light? *(No.)*

Now, if you want to see water move this way, you can spend sometime over at the Science Learning Center.

Learning Centers

Science Center

Supplies Needed: plastic tub to hold water, a variety of containers that will NOT float, some "sink and float" items, towels for cleanup, a large pitcher (or two) of water

1. Set all the containers in the empty tub.
2. Begin to pour the water at one end of the tub.
3. Ask the children to describe how the water is traveling.

> Is the water moving in a straight line? (No)
>
> What happens when the water runs into an obstacle? *(Goes around)*
>
> Water likes to go wherever it can, doesn't it?
>
> Now help me take out the containers that won't float.
>
> Let's put in the other items one at a time. Will they sink or float?

(Take turns adding items to tub. Remind children to keep the water in the tub. Let children experiment with items sinking and floating. Provide towels for cleanup.)

Older Children

Supplies Needed: file cards with words listing the ways we use water, your graph with the children's names, markers, a glass, a jar of tap water, plus a bottle of fresh water

Set the jar and bottle of water on the table. Invite children to help make a list about everything all of us do with water (draw pictures).

Discuss:
- God gave us lots of water. What did you find out about water this week?

- How important is water in your life?

- What do you do with water when you are getting ready for the day?

- What else do you use water for?

- What would happen if the earth had no water? What if you had no water? When have you ever been very thirsty?

Allow the children to discuss their ideas a while. Then graph the number of things each child has on his/her list of what can be done with water. The child with the longest list wins a prize— a bottle of fresh water!

Give each child a file card with a "water word" (faucet, shower, bath, tub, river, lake, glass of water, etc) on it. Give each child a turn to act out the word on his/her card and see if the others can guess.

Learning Centers

Art Center

Supplies Needed: construction paper, crayons, paintbrushes, blue wash (diluted blue tempera paint), a plastic tablecloth to protect floor or carpet

Have 3–5 children at a time draw crayon pictures on construction paper.
Explain:

- Today you can draw a picture of something you like to do with water.
- First draw your picture, but do not draw any water yet.
- We will paint the water on your picture when you are all finished.

Talk with children about their pictures as they are drawing, i.e.:

Do you like to go swimming? Who goes with you? Where do you go?

Is that a picture of your bathtub? Are there toys in your bathtub?

When the pictures are complete, give the children a paintbrush. Let them splash a little blue wash of tempera paint where the water should go on their paper. NOTE: the paint will not stick to crayons, only to plain construction paper.

Younger Children

Supplies Needed: use the Science Center and its supplies or set up a separate water table with plastic containers

Water play at today's science center will work very well with this age. However, it is often difficult for younger children to break into the play of older children, especially if the older children are having a good time.

One suggestion is to have a separate tub for the younger children. Another is to give them their own time at the Science Center water table.

Talk with the children about God making water for us, all the fun things we can do with water, where they have played in water (Beach, pool, lake, bathtub, etc.)

**Invite children to come to
Circle Time to join you.**

Circle Time Song

Review the first two verses of the "Creation Song."
Sing to the tune of "Frere Jacques" ("Are You Sleeping?").

On Day one, on Day one,
God did make, God did make
Light to shine in darkness,
Light to shine in darkness.
It was good. It was good.

On Day two, on Day two,
God did make, God did make
Lots of sky and water,
Lots of sky and water.
It was good. It was good.

Other Songs:

"Peace Like a River"
"Deep and Wide"
"The Raindrop Song"

* * *

God Made Water

Water above *(Hands over head)*
Water below *(Hands down low)*

God made the water *(Point to heaven)*
This I know. *(Point to own head)*

To drink, to clean, to grow, to play,
(Imitate each action as you say it)

God made water on the second day!
(Hold up two fingers)

Circle Time Discussion

Remember when we talked about the sky. What do you remember about the sky?
(The sky changes with the weather.)

Now we will talk about the water.
Which is bigger, the water or the sky? *(Sky)*
How do you know the sky is bigger?
(Sky extends way out into outer space, farther than we can see.)

God made the sky big enough and high enough for everyone on earth. Now look at a globe or map of the world. See all the water in the oceans of the earth?

But does everyone on earth have enough water? No. Some places are very dry, making it hard to grow food. These dry places are called a "desert." Only a few plants can live in a desert. Have any of you ever been in a "desert"? Would you like to live in a desert without any water? Why not?

Why do you think God made water? *(He loves us.)*
Why is water so important? *(Nothing can grow without water. All animals and plants would die without water. People can only live three or four days without drinking any water.)*

What different kinds of "water" can we find around where we live?
(Ocean, rivers, lakes, streams, underground springs, hot springs, ponds, puddles, water from our faucet, rain from the clouds, etc.)

God separated water above the earth from water on the earth. What kinds of water are on the ground of the earth? *(Oceans, rivers, lakes, streams, etc.)*

What kind of water is up in the sky?
(Clouds full of evaporated water)

What is your favorite thing about the water God made? *(Color of it, fun to swim in it, fun to splash in it, cools us off on a hot day, need water to make lemonade, need water to wash our bodies.)*
Aren't we THANKFUL for water God made?

Now let's practice our
Bible Memory Verse.

Practice the Memory Verse

"God said, Let the waters under the heaven be gathered together unto one place. . . God called the dry land Earth; and the gathering together of the waters called he Seas" (Genesis 1:9–10 KJV).

Explain: Watch me and do what I do.
We are going to practice this verse by also using our whole body.
When I say "gathered together into one place," then stretch your arms way out from your sides and pretend like you are pulling all the water into one place as you pull your arms together in front of you. Then I will say, "God called the waters that were gathered together . . . " and ALL of you will say the word: "SEAS"

(Can explain to children: "Seas" is another word for Ocean).

Post-Session Learning Centers

(After Circle Time, rotate children to another Learning Center)

Closing • Back to Circle Time

At the end of the class, gather the children together for a closing circle. Have the children tell what their favorite part of the day was.
Help them review each step.

Then pray together.

Dear God, we are thankful You love us. Thank You for making all the water in the oceans and in the clouds. We need water for so many things. Help us know how to take care of Earth's water so everyone will have enough. In Jesus' Name we pray. Amen.

Does anyone know what we will talk about next time? *(Land)*

Remember to send home Parent Page

Dear Parents,

Today was a busy day! We learned that God made water, and we talked about many of the ways we need it every day. We learned action–motions, built an obstacle course to show how water travels, and painted a water picture. Have your child sing the Creation Song to you and tell you what he or she liked best.

Next Time: We will talk about God making land. This will be a good week to dig in the dirt, allow your child to play in a sandbox, visit the beach, or plant a garden. Notice that "land" involves many kinds of dirt and rocks. Help your child find one really nice (and pretty small) rock he or she would like to bring to class next week.

Read: Genesis 1:9–10 with your child. Pray with your child. Thank God for rocks and land.

Bring next time: a pretty rock marked with your child's name. These will be sent home again.

For Parents: Rocks are solid and dependable ground on which to build. Be encouraged as you trust the Lord God, your strong rock, upon whom you can depend at all times.

Blessings to your family from our Teaching Staff

copy and distribute

Dear Parents,

Lesson 3

Today was a busy day! We learned that God made water, and we talked about many of the ways we need it every day. We learned action–motions, built an obstacle course to show how water travels, and painted a water picture. Have your child sing the Creation Song to you and tell you what he or she liked best.

Next Time: We will talk about God making land. This will be a good week to dig in the dirt, allow your child to play in a sandbox, visit the beach, or plant a garden. Notice that "land" involves many kinds of dirt and rocks. Help your child find one really nice (and pretty small) rock he or she would like to bring to class next week.

Read: Genesis 1:9–10 with your child. Pray with your child. Thank God for rocks and land.

Bring next time: a pretty rock marked with your child's name. These will be sent home again.

For Parents: Rocks are solid and dependable ground on which to build. Be encouraged as you trust the Lord God, your strong rock, upon whom you can depend at all times.

Blessings to your family from our Teaching Staff

God said, "Let the water under the heaven be gathered together unto one place and let the dry land appear: and it was so. And God saw that it was good" (Genesis 1:9–10 KJV).

Bubble Fun

Take a piece of cotton string about three to four feet long and tie the ends together so it forms a loop. Dip the whole thing into a dish of soap solution and stretch it out so you have a bubble film caught in the middle. Hold it up and blow gently to create hundreds of bubbles. Make just one bubble, then catch it on the bubble film and let it slide back and forth between your hands.

The very best bubble tools are cheap, easy to use, and you have them with you! They are your hands. Put your fingers together so they form an opening like the one in the picture to the left. Dip your hands in a bowl of bubble solution to get a bubble film. Blow gently to make bubbles up to two feet in diameter.

It is dryness, not sharpness, that pops bubbles. This means that if you get your bubble tools wet, you can touch a bubble without popping it. The girl in the photo to the left is able to hold a bubble because her hand is soaked with bubble solution.

God Creates LAND

"God said, Let the dry land appear, and it was so. God called the dry land Earth; And God saw that it was good" (Genesis 1:9-10 KJV).

Get Ready:

☐ **PRAY** throughout the week that God will bless you and your children with understanding of the awesome power of His creation.

☐ **MAKE COPIES** of the parent take-home page.

☐ **CONTACT ASSISTANTS** to remind them that you look forward to working with them. Go over the things you would like them to do in class.

☐ **PREPARE** — It may take a while to gather enough small plastic containers for the art project. If needed, contact class-room parents or neighbors to help collect a container for each child.

☐ **GATHER** *The Creation Story for Children* (optional) plus other materials for your centers and circle time.

Welcome parents and children as they arrive. Remember to call each one by name. Invite children to join one of the learning centers.

Learning Center Supplies

Physical Center
#1 — a plastic tablecloth to protect the floor, a tub of sand/dirt or potting soil, garden hand shovels, containers for filling and pouring out sand
#2 — rocks, masking tape

Science Center
magnifying glasses, many different kinds of rocks, small containers of water, eyedroppers, a small food scale and balance scale (to weigh and compare rocks)

Art Center
a small plastic container (empty butter, cream cheese or yogurt container) for each child, three colors of aquarium rocks, a lot of liquid glue, a bowl, and several sturdy spoons

Older/Younger Students
- a variety of rocks, plus several nails
- dirt (maybe some sand), rocks, scoops, spoons, buckets, containers

Learning Centers
(To involve children before and after Circle Time Learning)

Physical Center

Option #1

Supplies Needed: a plastic tablecloth to protect the floor, a tub of sand or dirt or potting soil, garden hand shovels (or old serving spoons) and containers for filling and pouring out the sand

- Set the tablecloth on the floor and set the tub on top of it.

- Allow three to five children at a time to explore the dirt by digging, filling up, and pouring out.

- You might want to add a little water.

Note: Resist the urge to add plants or anything that hasn't yet been "created" in our series. Water and rocks are fine.

Discuss:

Can you imagine what the world was like when there was only water, sand, and rocks?

What kinds of sounds do you think you would hear? *(Swishing, banging, bumping)*

It would be a lot like having a huge beach all around you, wouldn't it? But some things we find at the beach would be missing.

What would we miss seeing at the beach? *(There would be no plants, no fish, no birds, no seashells, and no animals yet.)*

Would you have liked to visit the beach when it was like that? Why or why not?

Physical Center

Option #2

Supplies Needed: a variety of rocks, plus masking tape. Write names on rocks if brought from different homes.

- Use masking tape to make two lines on the floor (three feet long) about five feet apart.
- Have the children each get a stone to hold as they stand behind one line.

Explain:
We are going to play a game to see who can toss their rock and get it closest to the other line.

1. Just toss your rock gently like this. *(Demonstrate a gentle toss)*

2. Place both of your feet behind the line. *(Demonstrate)*

3. The person who tosses his or her rock closest to the other line gets to go first when we play the game next time.

4. Let's remember to take turns. We will toss our rocks one at a time.

Learning Centers

Science Center

Supplies Needed: magnifying glasses, lots of rocks of various weights, sizes and colors, small containers of water, eyedroppers, a small food scale and a balance scale, some jewelry made from precious stones

Invite the children to compare the rocks and look at them with magnifying glasses.

Discuss:
- Which rocks are smooth?
- Which rocks are rough?
- Do you know what makes one rock smooth and another rough? *(Water, wind, a rock polisher)*

- What colors are the rocks?
- Does the color change if you put a little drop of water on the rocks?

(Demonstrate with a multi-colored rock.)

- Which rocks are heavy? Which rocks are lightweight? *(Compare on scales.)*
- Do you know what makes some rocks heavier than others? *(The materials that make up the rock are packed more tightly together in the heavy rock.)*
- God made many different kinds of rocks. Some rocks are very valuable, like gold, rubies, diamonds. *(Show jewelry or your ring with gold/diamond/gem stones.)*
- Which of these rocks are your favorite?

Older Children

Supplies Needed: a variety of rocks plus a NAIL for each child

Ask children to compare their rocks again. Some are rough, some are smooth, some are heavy, and some are light. Ask them to try to scratch their rocks with the nails.

Some rocks may be easy to scratch. Others may be nearly impossible to scratch. Give them a few minutes to compare their results.

- What did you find out about your rocks? Are they all the same?
- Can you think of anything people could do with rocks?

  Some ancient people used rocks to scratch pictures on cave walls. Those pictures helped show us something about how they lived years ago.

- Which rocks do you think would be good for drawing pictures?
- Which would not? What else could you do with rocks? *(Build "fences" put in yards)*

Learning Centers

Art Center

NOTE: This art project can be done as a large group exercise or as a center activity. Make sure to supervise this activity.

Supplies Needed: a small plastic container (an empty yogurt, cream cheese, or butter container) for each child, three colors of aquarium rocks, and a lot of liquid glue, a bowl, and sturdy spoons

Work with three or four children at a time.

1. In a bowl, mix the aquarium rocks with glue until the consistency is like wet concrete.

2. Let children take turns spooning the mixture into their plastic containers.

3. They should fill the container only about halfway to the top.

NOTE: If you have room to store the containers until next week when the glue is completely dry, then you will cut and peel off the container next week. Otherwise send them home with the children. The Parent Page will include instructions on what to be done with the project when it has finally dried.

Younger Children

Supplies Needed: dirt (maybe some sand), rocks, scoops, spoons, buckets, containers

Sensory activities work very well at this age.
Allow younger children their own time at the dirt table.

While they are playing, discuss the kinds of "land" God has made for us:

* Where have YOU found dirt? Do you have dirt in your backyard?
  In a nearby park? in the country? on a farm? in your garden?

* Why do you think God made so much dirt?

* What can you do with dirt? *(Dig, plant seeds, pile up mounds of dirt, etc.)*

* Do you like the way dirt feels? *(Include clumps of dirt, mud, garden dirt, etc.)*

* What about sand? Where do you find it? Do you like dirt or sand better?

**Invite children to come to
Circle Time to join you.**

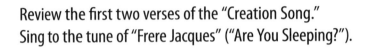

Circle Time Song

Review the first two verses of the "Creation Song."
Sing to the tune of "Frere Jacques" ("Are You Sleeping?").

On Day one, on Day one,

God did make, God did make

Light to shine in darkness,

Light to shine in darkness.

It was good. It was good.

On Day two, on Day two,

God did make, God did make

Lots of sky and water,

Lots of sky and water.

It was good. It was good.

*   *   *

Other Songs:

"The Solid Rock

"Everything Is Possible"

"The Wise Man Built . . . upon the Rock"

Circle Time Discussion

What did God make on Day 3 ? *(Land, Earth)*

God made the water go into certain areas so there would be some dry land for us. Today many kinds of "land" are all around us and under our feet.

Can you name some kinds of land you have walked on? *(Sandy beaches, rocky hills and mountains, dirt hillsides, sandy deserts, etc.)*

What kind of land do we find on the beaches? *(Sand, sand dunes, pebbles, rocks)*

What do we find in the mountains? *(Big rocks, huge boulders, small rocks, dirt)*

What kind of land do did God made for our own yards? *(Dirt, gravel, stones, and rocks of all sizes)*

WHAT is your favorite kind of land?
WHY is it your favorite land?

If we try very hard, could any of us make some rocks like God did?
(No. Only God can make rocks!)

God not only made rocks, God made LOTS of different kinds of rocks! Some rocks have very beautiful colors in them.

What did God say about the land when it was first created? *(God said it was good!)*

Could people live on the Earth if there wasn't any dry land? No. We need land to walk on, land on which to build a house, land to give us a place to grow our food, land to play on the grass and to run on the beach.

What would happen if we had to live in the ocean? Do you think we could live on the ocean water all the time? *(Maybe, if we had a great big boat. But we would still need food that only grows on the land.)*

Could we live up in the air all the time?

Let's be thankful God loves us and made lots of LAND for us. Plants and animals couldn't live very long without land. And all of us couldn't live long without land.

Now let's practice our Bible Memory Verse.

Practice the Memory Verse

"God called the dry ground Earth... And God saw that it was good"
(Genesis 1:9–10 KJV).

Make the memory verse into a fingerplay, with hand motions:

God called	*(Cup hands as if calling)*
the dry ground	*(Rub hands horizontally)*
Earth.	*(Hands down on either side)*
God saw that	*(Place hand above eyes)*
it was good!	*(Hug self)*
(Genesis 1:9–10)	NOTE: Repeat together until children learn it.

Post-Session Learning Centers

(After Circle Time, rotate children to another Learning Center)

Closing • Back to Circle Time

At the end of the class, gather the children together for a closing circle. Have the children tell what their favorite part of the day was.
Help them review each step.

Then pray together.
"Thank You, God, for making so many kinds of dry land for us to enjoy. Teach us how to take good care of the wonderful world You made. Thank You for Your love. Thank You for our Earth. Amen."

Next week we will learn about something else God made for us to enjoy. Can you guess what it is? *(Plants, trees, and food)*

Remember to send home Parent Page

Dear Parents,

Today: We learned about the rocks, sand, and dirt God made. We compared our rocks by size, weight, color, and texture. We weighed them, tossed them, and tried to scratch them. If your child brought home a container of rocks and glue, please let it dry a few days. Then cut the container and peel it away. It's a reminder, in THREE colors, of what God made on Day 3.

Next Time: We will study the different plants God made. Why not take a field trip through the produce department or a local fruit stand this week? Talk about the different kinds of plants God made for our enjoyment. Try eating a new fruit or vegetable you've never eaten!

Read: Genesis 1:11–13 with your child. Pray with your child, thanking God for all of the colorful, fascinating, and great–tasting plants in the world.

Bring Next Time: a fruit or vegetable to contribute to a salad for the class snack.
(NOTE: Please let us know if your child is allergic to any foods.)

For Parents: God certainly gave us a wonderful variety of colorful plants for our pleasure and enjoyment. Thank God for the great variety of things we can use and enjoy.

Blessings to your family from our Teaching Staff

copy and distribute

Dear Parents,

Lesson 4

Today: We learned about the rocks, sand, and dirt God made. We compared our rocks by size, weight, color, and texture. We weighed them, tossed them, and tried to scratch them. If your child brought home a container of rocks and glue, please let it dry a few days. Then cut the container and peel it away. It's a reminder, in THREE colors, of what God made on Day 3.

Next Time: We will study the different plants God made. Why not take a field trip through the produce department or a local fruit stand this week? Talk about the different kinds of plants God made for our enjoyment. Try eating a new fruit or vegetable you've never eaten!

Read: Genesis 1:11–13 with your child. Pray with your child, thanking God for all of the colorful, fascinating, and great–tasting plants in the world.

Bring Next Time: a fruit or vegetable to contribute to a salad for the class snack.
(NOTE: Please let us know if your child is allergic to any foods.)

For Parents: God certainly gave us a wonderful variety of colorful plants for our pleasure and enjoyment. Thank God for the great variety of things we can use and enjoy.

Blessings to your family from our Teaching Staff

God Creates LAND

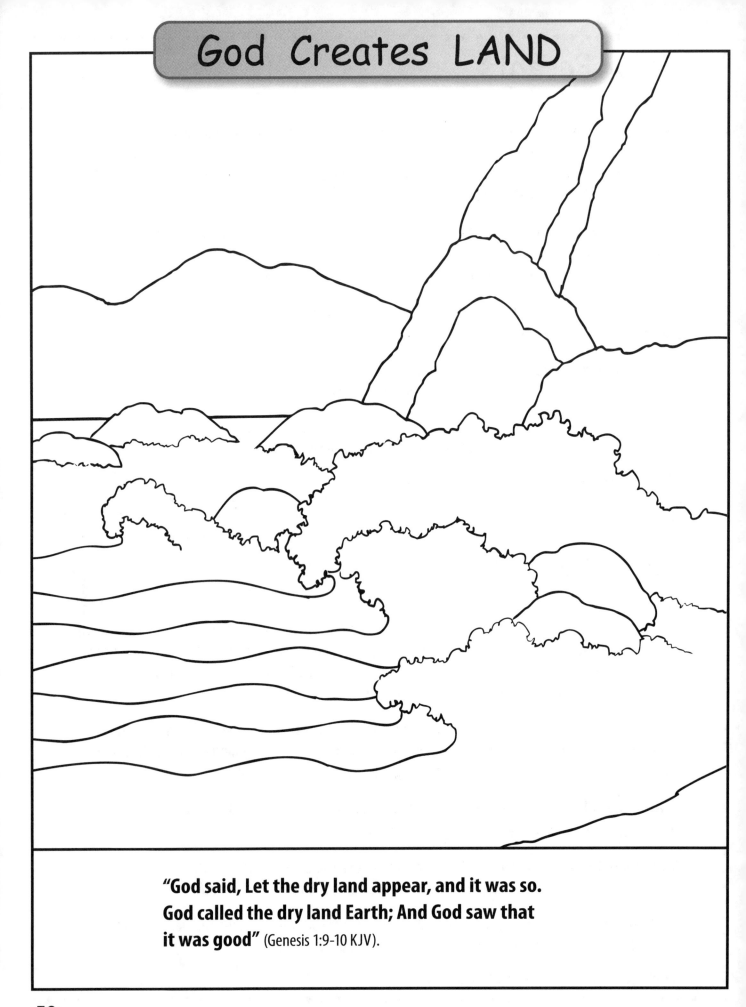

"God said, Let the dry land appear, and it was so. God called the dry land Earth; And God saw that it was good" (Genesis 1:9-10 KJV).

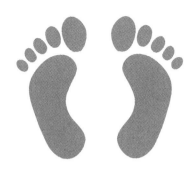

Our FEET need LAND

Supplies Needed: a large space in which to have children sitting in a circle

If there was only WATER and no LAND, what would we do?
We couldn't walk on the water, just like we can't walk on the air around us.
We'd have to swim all the time or ride in a boat.
Would you like that?
How could we live if we had to swim all the time?

We need LAND so we can live!
We need LAND so our feet can STAND on it.

Okay, now let's all STAND UP with our feet on the ground—land.

Now I need your help in thinking about all the things we do on land.

We WALK on land. Sometimes we walk in the dirt, or on a sandy beach, or on a rocky mountain. Let's lift our feet up and down and pretend to walk. (Walk.)

We RUN on land. Let's move our feet really fast and pretend to run on the land.

We JUMP on land. Let's see how high we can jump on land. Jump, jump, jump.

We SKIP on land. Let's skip around in a circle on the land.

We TIP–TOE on land. Let's all quietly tip–toe around in a circle.

We SIT on land. Let's sit down on the land.

We sometimes LIE DOWN on the ground. Let's all lie down right now.
Let's thank God together. "Thank You, dear God, for all the LAND You made for us."

God Creates PLANTS

"And God said, 'Let the bring forth grass, the herb yielding seed, and the fruit tree yielding fruit after his kind. . . and it was so. . . and God saw that it was good" (Genesis 1:11–13 KJV).

Welcome parents and children as they arrive.
Remember to call each one by name.
Invite children to join one of the learning centers.

Get Ready:

☐ **PRAY** throughout the week that God will bless you and your children with understanding of the awesome power of His creation.

☐ **MAKE COPIES** of the parent take-home page (for a group class).

☐ **CONTACT ASSISTANTS**

Go over the things you would like them to do in class.

☐ **PREPARE**

- Secure two adult volunteers to help make the salads.
- Separate seeds from five—six seed packets. Place in separate plastic baggies for a matching game.
- Cut two—three vegetables crosswise to use in painting. Put two—three colors of washable paint in pie tins.

☐ **GATHER** *The Creation Story for Children* (optional) plus other materials for your centers and circle time.

Learning Center Supplies

Physical Center
a variety of fruits and vegetables

Science Center
#1 – vegetable peelers, plastic knives, two large bowls, small paper bowls, and plastic spoons or forks
(Extra fruit/veggies for those who do not bring some.)
#2 – packets of seeds and plastic bags for seeds
#3 – plastic cups, potting soil, scoop or old spoons, seeds, craft sticks, marker

Art Center
construction paper, two to three colors of tempera paint (pie plates for the paint), vegetables you cut up ahead of time, baby wipes

Older/Younger Students
- colored markers, drawing paper
- half sheets of light–blue construction paper, glue sticks, a variety of precut paper flowers and stems

Learning Centers

(To involve children before and after Circle Time Learning)

Physical Center

Supplies Needed: a variety of fruits and veggies

Let each child select a fruit or vegetable. Assign them the name of what they pick. *(Try to hand out a variety of fruit or veggies.)*

1. Have all the children stand in a circle.

2. Call out names of fruits and vegetables in random order. *(Pears, apples, grapes, bananas, kiwis, mangos, oranges, blueberries, grapefruit, cabbage, tomato, carrot, cucumber, etc.)*

EXPLAIN:
When you hear the name of the fruit or vegetable you are holding, it is your signal to run around the outside of the circle and then come back to your original spot.

NOTE: Be sure to call names of all the fruits and vegetables children are holding. Also include names of foods that are not as well known. Be prepared to tell children about the lesser-known foods if they should ask.

Science Center

Option #1

Supplies Needed: vegetable peelers, plastic knives, two large bowls, small paper bowls, plastic spoons or forks, wax paper or cutting board (Extra fruit/veggies for children who didn't bring some.)

With supervision, this center can be done with preschoolers. Let children decide if the food they pick is a fruit or vegetable. Have one station set up for each. At the stations, let your volunteers help children prepare a fruit salad or a vegetable salad. Be sure children wash hands. Set out wax paper and/or cutting boards. Older children can use the peelers with care. Most children can use a plastic knife to chop up foods such as grapes and bananas. While preparing the salads, keep a running dialogue with the children about the foods.

Discuss:
- Carrots are great! They taste good and they are good for your eyes. Do you like them better raw or cooked?

- What is your favorite fruit? These grapes look delicious. Let's cut each one in half with our plastic knives.

- Are there any seeds inside the grape?
- Are there seeds inside the banana?

Let's compare seeds. Slice a pear and find the seeds inside. I'll cut this apple through the center so we can see apple seeds. Do you see a star shape INside this apple? Where are the strawberry's seeds? *(On the OUTside of the fruit)*

Salads can be shared right away, or set aside for your regular snack time. Enjoy the flavors!

NOTE: Be careful—Nut allergies are dangerous! Do NOT include any nuts in this study of plants. Be aware of any other allergies before class.

Learning Centers

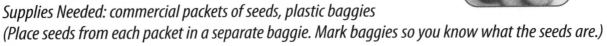

CARROT

Science Center

Option #2

Supplies Needed: commercial packets of seeds, plastic baggies
(Place seeds from each packet in a separate baggie. Mark baggies so you know what the seeds are.)

Explain: This is a matching game.
See the packets with pictures on them.
Each seed will grow into a plant like this. Now let's try to match the picture to the seeds from inside each pack.

- Do you know what this is? This is a _____.
  Have you eaten this before?

- Do you like how it tastes? Can you find the seeds that match with the picture of this plant? *(Repeat this process with all of the seeds. Notice the intricate varieties of seeds.)*

- God made a lot of different plants, didn't He? There are thousands of plants.

- The Bible tells us God made plants for us to enjoy. In what other ways are plants good for us?

(Plants make good homes for birds and animals. Trees help make homes for us. Plants put oxygen in the air for us to breath. Plants taste good and help our bodies grow. Some plants make the ground rich in nutrients, etc.)

- Some plants we enjoy by eating them.
- Some of them are good for looking at.
- But some plants would make us very sick. So always check with your parents before you eat something new.

Art Center

Supplies Needed: construction paper, two or three colors of tempera paint (pie plates work well for this painting activity), the vegetables that you cut up ahead of time, baby wipes

- Invite children to join you at the art table. Demonstrate how to dip the vegetables in the paint and scrape the extra paint off on the edge of the pie plate.

- Make a print of the vegetable, then make a series of prints on the paper.

- Allow three to four children to paint their vegetable prints at a time.
  Talk about the wonderful plants God made for us to eat and to enjoy.

(Note: If the paint is mostly scraped on the side of the pie plate, you will find the prints are more dramatic and will dry more quickly.)

Learning Centers

Science Center

Option #3

Supplies Needed: plastic cups, potting soil, scoop/old spoon, seeds, craft sticks with names of children on them, marker

1. Invite the children to print their name on one of the craft sticks. Set aside.

2. Let them use a scoop or old spoon to fill the cup half full of potting soil.

3. Then put four or five seeds in the cup. Finish filling cup with potting soil.

4. Put the craft stick with their name on it in the cup to take home.

5. Talk about how God waters seeds by sending rain. Explain how they can the seeds they take home. *(Water gently; don't flood the cup, etc.)*

Older Children

Supplies Needed: none

Older children will be intrigued by the activities today. If they finish early, ask them to help out at one of the stations or help clean up.

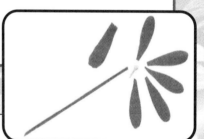

Younger Children

Supplies Needed: half–sheets of light–blue construction paper, glue sticks, a variety of pre-cut paper flowers and petals of different colors, plus several green paper "stems" for each child (can use leaves in the Fall).

1. Give each child a piece of blue construction paper and a glue stick.

2. Allow children to choose a variety of paper stems and flower cut–outs. Help them notice all the colors.

3. Using a sample, show children how to glue the flower stems on the paper first. Then glue the flower shapes at the top of the stem.

4. Discuss: Which colors of flowers do you like best? Which shapes of flowers do you like best? Which plants are your favorites?

Aren't you glad God loves us and was good to give us trees and beautiful flowers? Let's be sure to thank God for all the plants and trees and flowers we enjoy every day.

Invite children to come to Circle Time to join you.

Circle Time Song

Review the first two verses of the "Creation Song."
Teach verse three.
Sing to the tune of "Frere Jacques" (Are You Sleeping?).

On Day one, on Day one,
God did make, God did make
Light to shine in darkness,
Light to shine in darkness.
It was good. It was good.

On Day two, on Day two,
God did make, God did make
Lots of sky and water,
Lots of sky and water.
It was good. It was good.

On Day three, on Day three,
God did make, God did make
Many trees and flowers,
Many trees and flowers.
It was good. It was good

* * *

Other Songs:

"Everything Is Possible"

"He's Got the Whole World"

Circle Time Discussion

God made land on Day 3. Then God made something wonderful grow on the land. What was it? *(Lots of plants.)*

Look at all the kinds of plants—WOW! Do you see what's in the different rows? Here is a row for nuts and grain. Here is a row for fruits, and another row for vegetables.

Which kinds of fruits and vegetables did we use in our salads today? Which fruits are your favorite? Which vegetables?

What is in this row? *(Flowers)* Which flowers are your favorite? Which flowers grow in your yard?

Why do you suppose God made so many flowers? *(They are beautiful and colorful. Flowers cheer us up and make our homes and yards look beautiful.)*

What else do you see here? *(Allow children time to look and respond.)*

Look at all the trees God made! Which trees do you see where you live? It would be hard to count every plant on these pages, wouldn't it?

All of these flowers and trees are only a few of the thousands of plants God made.

Why do you think God made so many kinds of plants?
(God made plants do great things to help us grow and live. Many plants are good for us to eat. Some plants give off oxygen for us to breathe. Plants help us grow strong and stay healthy. People couldn't live without plants.)

Look inside each plant. Do you see the little seeds God made? Every tiny seed can grow into another big plant just like its "parent" plant.

How does a little seed know to grow up into a sunflower or a daisy? Isn't it fun and amazing how God helps little seeds know how to grow?

Could people grow any plants without seeds? No! God thought of everything. God loves us very much to give us so many tasty and pretty plants.

Now let's practice our Bible Memory Verse.

Practice the Memory Verse

And God said, 'Let the earth bring forth [plants]. Let them bear their own seeds...
and God saw that it was good (Genesis 1:11–12 paraphrase).

Tell the children: I am so excited about what God made! I want to tell my grandma.
Do you want to tell your grandma too? Get your telephone.
(Place your thumb and pinkie finger up to your face, then "dial" the number.)

Hi, Grandma! Do you know what God did on Day Three? I learned a memory verse about it: "God said, 'Let the earth bring forth [plants]. Let them bear their own seeds' . . . God saw that it was good" (Genesis 1:11-12).

Now YOU think of someone else to call and tell them what God did!
Continue until children easily repeat the verse or until they run out of people to phone.

Post-Session Learning Centers

(After Circle Time, rotate children to another Learning Center)

Closing • Back to Circle Time

At the end of the class, gather the children together for a closing circle. Let children tell about their favorite part of the day. Help them review each step.

Then pray together.
Thank You, God, for making such good food for us to eat. Thank You for all the pretty plants and tall trees for us to enjoy every day. We're glad You love us and take good care of us by giving us plants. Amen.

Next Time we will learn about something else God made for us to enjoy. Can anyone guess what it is? *(Sun, moon, stars)*

Remember to send home Parent Page

Dear Parents,

Today: We had a busy day exploring plants. Thank you for sending a fruit or vegetable with your child. We made great–tasting salads out of them! We also painted with vegetables and matched seeds with a picture of what the seeds would become. Have your child sing the Creation Song to you and tell you what he/she liked best about our class today.

Next Time: We will take a little trip to outer space and talk about God creating the sun, moon, and stars. If you live in an area where it is easy to see the stars in the night sky, take 10 or 15 minutes outside with your child. Sit or lie on a blanket in the grass and look up. Talk about what you see in the vast universe around our planet.

Read: Genesis 1:14–19 with your child. Pray with your child. Thank God for making all of the wonderful stars, the sun, and the moon for us to enjoy and to light up our day and night.

Bring Next Time: a smile

For Parents: When did you last take time to stop and look up into the night skies? Let the wondrous display of billions of stars and galaxies declare the glory of God and His love to you.

Blessings to your family from our Teaching Staff

copy and distribute

Dear Parents,

Lesson 5

Today: We had a busy day exploring plants. Thank you for sending a fruit or vegetable with your child. We made great–tasting salads out of them! We also painted with vegetables and matched seeds with a picture of what the seeds would become. Have your child sing the Creation Song to you and tell you what he/she liked best about our class today.

Next Time: We will take a little trip to outer space and talk about God creating the sun, moon, and stars. If you live in an area where it is easy to see the stars in the night sky, take 10 or 15 minutes outside with your child. Sit or lie on a blanket in the grass and look up. Talk about what you see in the vast universe around our planet.

Read: Genesis 1:14–19 with your child. Pray with your child. Thank God for making all of the wonderful stars, the sun, and the moon for us to enjoy and to light up our day and night.

Bring Next Time: a smile

For Parents: When did you last take time to stop and look up into the night skies? Let the wondrous display of billions of stars and galaxies declare the glory of God and His love to you.

Blessings to your family from our Teaching Staff

"And God said, 'Let the bring forth grass, the herb yielding seed, and the fruit tree yielding fruit after his kind... and it was so... and God saw that it was good" (Genesis 1:11-13 KJV).

Thank You, God, for PLANTS

Supplies Needed: Fill a platter with each of the food items listed below.
Hold up both handfuls of fingers.

What if you had only TWO things to eat? . . . like onions & cabbage?
Aren't you glad God made LOTS of yummy fruits and veggies?

Thank You, dear God, for:

 **ONE** sweet Pineapple

TWO juicy Oranges

 **THREE** black Avocados

FOUR red Tomatoes

 FIVE crunchy Walnuts

SIX green Apples

 **SEVEN** brown Potatoes

EIGHT yellow Bananas

 **NINE** round Blueberries

TEN purple Grapes

Notice the variety of colors God made.
Cut an apple in half horizontally.
See the seed star pattern inside.
Cut other food items apart to look inside.

God Made Flowers

Supplies Needed: one or two long–stemmed white carnations, a clear glass vase, green food coloring

1. Make a fresh diagonal cut on the end of carnation.
2. Place the carnation in a clear glass vase of water.
3. Have children watch as you add a drops of green food color.
4. Place the flower/vase where children can see it.

Observe the flower during the day and also on the following days.
Watch for changes in the color of the flower.

Talk with the children about what happens to the flower.

- Notice how the flower stem has veins which carry water from the roots up to the flower petals.

- Notice the capillary action when the colored water moves up the stem and into veins of the petals.

Play Dough Flowers

Supplies Needed: play dough of various colors, wax paper on which to form the flowers, cloth or paper towels, and a basin of soapy water for clean–up

- Form a ball of the play dough for the center of the flower.

- Flatten out the ball to make the flower's center.

- Form smaller balls. Flatten them to make petals on your flower.

- Use some green play dough to make a stem and some leaves.

Pin a Petal on the Flower

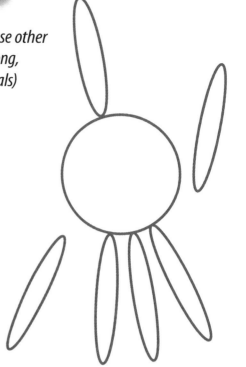

Supplies Needed: large sheet of yellow construction paper, use other colored construction paper to cut out "petals" about a foot long, scissors, tape, marker (to write children's names on their petals)

1. Cut our a 10 –12 inch yellow circle.

2. Tape circle on the wall at height of children's heads.

3. Give each child a petal with his or her name on it.

4. Blindfold children. Let them try to tape their petals at the edge of the center of the flower.

5. Let children take several turns.

Sorting Flowers

Supplies Needed: a low table, an assortment of plastic flowers; or use real flowers if they are available; several vases or pots in which to place the flowers

1. Lay out the flowers on a low table where children can see and reach them.
2. Talk about the differences in the flowers.
3. Let children decide how they want to sort and divide up the flowers.
(Can divide the children in groups of two or three to decide on what to do.)

> Do you want to put different kinds of flowers in one vase?
> Do you want to put flowers of different colors in one vase?
> Do you want to put flowers of the same color together?

Let the children talk about the bouquets and which they like best.
Set out the vases to be enjoyed by all.
Remind children how creative God is to make so many beautiful plants for us to enjoy.

God Creates SUN, MOON, STARS, & PLANETS

"And God said, Let there be lights... to divide the day from the night; and let them be for signs, and for seasons... And let them... give light upon the earth ... and God saw that it was good" (Genesis 1:16–18 KJV).

Welcome parents and children as they arrive.
Remember to call each one by name.
Invite children to join one of the learning centers.

Get Ready:

☐ **PRAY** throughout the week that God will bless you and your children with understanding of the awesome power of His creation.

☐ **MAKE COPIES** of the parent take-home page (for a group class).

☐ **CONTACT ASSISTANTS** Go over the things you would like them to do in class.

☐ **PREPARE** your Science learning center with sky–maps or "maps" of constellations or other pictures of the universe and its galaxies. On a wall or blackboard, place glow in the dark stars in a variety of formations: triangles, squares, rectangles, circles, a snake, etc.

☐ **GATHER** *The Creation Story for Children* (optional) plus other materials for your centers and circle time.

Learning Center Supplies

Physical Center
#1 – can show a poster or pictures of the moon
#2 – none

Science Center
#1 – sunshine (or a flashlight) and several 3–D objects
#2 – glow in the dark stars, pictures of constellations

Art Center
black or blue construction paper, star stickers, white or yellow chalk

Older/Younger Students
- blue or black construction paper, chalk, star stickers
- half sheets of black or blue construction paper, sponges cut in the shape of stars, crescent moons, and/or circles, white and yellow tempera paint, pie tins, paint smocks or shirts, water and towels

Learning Centers

(To involve children before and after Circle Time Learning)

Physical Center

Option #1

Supplies Needed: none (or show a poster of the moon or a picture of it from a book)

As the children stand in a circle around you, pretend to go on a MOONWALK.

Explain: Today we are going to pretend to be astronauts who fly to the moon. What will we need? *(Rocket, spacesuit, etc)*

As ideas come up, have the children pretend to step into a spacesuit and pull it on, climb up steps into the rocket, strap on their seatbelt, and then *blast off!*

Point out some of the constellations as you zoom past them in space.

Landing on the moon can be very exciting if you have a near miss of an asteroid or some other pretend emergency. Finally have the children land, unstrap their seatbelts, climb out of the spaceship and down the ladder, and begin to walk on the moon.

What is it like to walk on the moon? Is it the same as the earth? Why or why not? *(The moon has less gravity than earth, so you can jump higher and bounce higher.)*

Does the moon have light like the earth? Does the moon have water or plants? (No) Would you like to live on the moon? Why or why not? *(Then return to earth.)*

Physical Learning Center, Option #2 — Shadow Tag

- If the day is sunny, have one adult take the children outside to play "shadow tag."
- Show them the shadow made by their bodies blocking the sunlight.
- Instead of tagging each other's bodies, ask them to tag each other's *shadows!*

Science Center

Supplies Needed: sunshine (or a flashlight) and several 3–D objects

On a sunny day, take children outdoors to see how the sun makes shadows.

1. Show how a shadow is formed when something interrupts the straight line of the light coming from the sun. Talk about God's gift to us of the sun for light and heat and energy. What would the world be like without the sun? *(COLD and DARK)*

2. If you do NOT have sunny weather, use a flashlight and several 3–D objects to demonstrate the concept of light shining in a straight line with resulting shadows.

3. After several demonstrations, let the children predict the length of the shadow and what it will look like. Check the predictions to find out if they were correct.

Learning Centers

Science Center

Option #3

Supplies Needed: glow in the dark stars, for images of constellations see nasa.gov

Turn off lights. Invite children to look at your constellation pictures. Ask if they have looked through a telescope or been to a planetarium.

Explain:

Long ago, when some people looked at the stars, they thought some arrangements of stars looked a lot like things we see here on earth. Constellations are names for groups of stars in the sky that look like certain shapes.

(Examples: big dipper, little dipper, the bear, Leo the Lion, Orion, etc.)

- Give children time to look at pictures.

- Ask if they can find any constellations in the room.

- Go on your own "Star Search" until all constellations in the room are found.

Older Children

Supplies Needed: black or blue construction paper, chalk, and star stickers (use pictures of constellations, website images from the Science learning center or off the internet.)

Explain:
This activity is very similar to the art activity with one important exception. You will put <u>your own stars</u> on the paper.

Use your imaginations to come up with a picture for your constellation just as the early scientists did.

The scientists did not place stars in the sky where they wanted them. Scientists had to use the stars the way God gave them to us, in certain places in the sky.

1. So, put on your thinking cap and imagine what YOUR stars will form.

2. Then place some of your stars on your paper to make a certain shape.

3. Now connect the star–dots with your chalk. See if your friends can guess what you have made. You don't have to use all of your stickers for just one constellation.

NOTE: Encourage children to go out at night with their parents and look for constellations

Learning Centers

Art Center

NOTE: This art project can be done as a large group exercise or as a center activity.

Supplies Needed: black or blue construction paper, star stickers, white or yellow chalk

** Remind children about the constellations from Science Center Option #3.

- Today we are going to make up our own constellations.
- Think of something you want to draw in the sky. Then draw it with chalk.
- At some corners or parts of your drawings, place a star sticker.
- When you are done, you can draw in the moon if you want.

  Do you want to add the sun to your star picture? Why or why not?

If children have trouble understanding what you want them to do, show a simple example. *(A circle or square or triangle.)* Allow children to do as many constellations as they want as long as supplies last and everyone has a chance to make at least one art project of their own.

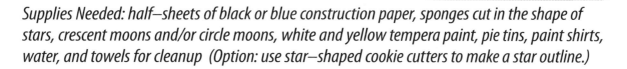

Younger Children

Supplies Needed: half—sheets of black or blue construction paper, sponges cut in the shape of stars, crescent moons and/or circle moons, white and yellow tempera paint, pie tins, paint shirts, water, and towels for cleanup (Option: use star—shaped cookie cutters to make a star outline.)

1. Work with two—three children at a time as you show them what to do with sponges:
   how to gently dip their sponge—stars in the paint
   how to scrape excess paint off the sponge onto the edge of the pie plate
   then how to stamp the sponge—star on their paper to make a print

2. Allow children to paint as many images on their paper as they like, and in any order. *(If you have different size sponges or other shapes, let children share.)*

3. Write the children's names on their paintings. Set papers aside to dry.

4. Have someone ready to help children clean up when they finish painting.

**Invite children to come to
Circle Time to join you.**

Circle Time Song

Review the first three verses of the "Creation Song."
Teach verse four.
Sing to the tune of "Frere Jacques" ("Are You Sleeping?").

On Day one, on Day one,
God did make, God did make
Light to shine in darkness,
Light to shine in darkness.
It was good. It was good.

On Day two, on Day two,
God did make, God did make
Lots of sky and water,
Lots of sky and water.
It was good. It was good.

On Day three, on Day three,
God did make, God did make
Many trees and flowers,
Many trees and flowers.
It was good. It was good.

On Day four, on Day four,
God did make, God did make
Sun and moon and stars,
Sun and moon and stars.
It was good. It was good.

Other Songs:

"This Little Light of Mine"
"Heavenly Sunshine"
"Twinkle, Twinkle, Little Star"
"Day by Day"

Circle Time Discussion

By now, the children should be telling *you* what is on the pages you already covered.

Look at all the stars and planets! Remember, "In the beginning God created the heaven and the earth."

What do you see in the picture?
Do you see the Earth where we live?
(Point to the bottom center of picture)

Can you find other planets in the heavens that circle the sun like the Earth does? *(Saturn with its rings and the reddish planet named Mars.)*

Can you see the sun? Where is it?
(Point to lower left corner)

Do you see our moon? Where is it?
(Between sun and earth)

What are all these swirling circles?
(They are called galaxies. The galaxy swirls are full of millions of stars and planets. They are all very, very far away from us.)

Do you know that the Earth is right in the middle of one of these galaxies?
Our galaxy is called the "Milky Way."

These galaxies look kind of "milky," don't they? The stars give a milky look. Each little white spot is actually a star!

Can people count all of the stars in the sky? *(No! If you counted one star every second of your whole life, you still would NOT be finished counting them even after 100 years!)*

Sometimes people make maps of the sky. Sailors used to look at the stars to find their way across the ocean at night. We can find directions from the stars. We can find the direction of North by finding the North Star in the sky. It is a very bright star. Have you ever seen it?

Our loving God made an big universe for us to enjoy. God also gave us the stars so we can find our way.

Now let's practice our Bible Memory Verse.

Practice the Memory Verse

*"God made two great lights. . . [God] made the stars also. . .
and God saw that it was good"* (Genesis 1:16-18 KJV).

- Divide the children into THREE groups. Designate one to be the sun, one to be the moon, and one to be the stars.

- As you repeat the verse together, have the sun and moon groups stand up and say, "God made two great lights."

- Then the third group will stand and say, "God also made the stars."

- Then everyone stands to say, "God saw that it was good" (Genesis 1:16–18).

Post-Session Learning Centers

(After Circle Time, rotate children to another Learning Center)

Closing • Back to Circle Time

At the end of the class, gather the children together for a closing circle. Let the children tell what their favorite part of the day was.
Help them review each step.

Then pray together:
Thank You, God, for making the sun to keep us warm. Thank You for making the moon and stars to shine at night. Thanks for making everything so good. We pray in Jesus' Name. Amen.

Do you know if God made something else after making the sun, moon, and stars? I can't wait to find out next time!

Remember to send home Parent Page

Dear Parents,

Today: We took a "trip" to the moon, created constellations, played shadow tag, and learned that God always helps us find our way. God loves us very much. Have your child sing the first four verses of the Creation Song to you and tell you what he/she liked best about class today.

Next Time: Our adventures will take us underwater, and we will talk about the fish and sea creatures God made. This would be a good week to visit a local aquarium or pet store to begin to get an idea of the variety of God's sea creatures. If you don't have a pet store nearby, perhaps you can check out a book with pictures of fish at the library.

Read: Genesis 1:20–22 with your child. Pray with your child, thanking God for His wonderful imagination and design in making all of the different sea creatures for us to enjoy.

Bring Next Time: a seashell

For Parents: Let your study of God's water creatures make you smile. Some of them are funny and imaginative. Let all creation reinforce your assurance of God's love and care.

Blessings to your family from our Teaching Staff

copy and distribute

Dear Parents,

Lesson 6

Today: We took a "trip" to the moon, created constellations, played shadow tag, and learned that God always helps us find our way. God loves us very much. Have your child sing the first four verses of the Creation Song to you and tell you what he/she liked best about class today.

Next Time: Our adventures will take us underwater, and we will talk about the fish and sea creatures God made. This would be a good week to visit a local aquarium or pet store to begin to get an idea of the variety of God's sea creatures. If you don't have a pet store nearby, perhaps you can check out a book with pictures of fish at the library.

Read: Genesis 1:20–22 with your child. Pray with your child, thanking God for His wonderful imagination and design in making all of the different sea creatures for us to enjoy.

Bring Next Time: a seashell

For Parents: Let your study of God's water creatures make you smile. Some of them are funny and imaginative. Let all creation reinforce your assurance of God's love and care.

Blessings to your family from our Teaching Staff

"And God said, Let there be lights... to divide the day from the night; and let them be for signs, and for seasons.... And let them... give light upon the earth" (Genesis 1:16—18 KJV).

Make Hand Shadows

Supplies Needed: a white wall or a white sheet, a bright lamp

Dog

Panther

Turkey

Goose

Rabbit

Kangaroo

God Creates SEA CREATURES

"God said, 'Let the waters bring forth abundantly the moving creatures'... and God created great whales... after their kind... And God blessed them, saying, Be fruitful, and multiply, and fill the waters in the sea" (Genesis 1:20-22 KJV).

Get Ready:

☐ **PRAY** throughout the week that God will bless you and your children with understanding of the awesome power of His creation.

☐ **MAKE COPIES** of the parent take-home page (for a group class).

☐ **CONTACT ASSISTANTS** Go over the things you would like them to do in class.

☐ **PREPARE** a tub filled with warm water for seashells in the Science Learning Center. Also shop for a whole fish to make a fish print in the Art Learning Center.

☐ **GATHER** *The Creation Story for Children* (optional) plus seashells and other materials for your learning centers.

Welcome parents and children as they arrive.
Remember to call each one by name.
Invite children to join one of the learning centers.

Learning Center Supplies

Physical Center
none

Science Center
#1 – seashells and/or plastic sea creatures, a tub of water, a plastic tablecloth, and towels
#2 – place five–eight seashells on a tray, sand dollar, a cloth

Art Center
a small whole fish or two from the local market, slightly diluted tempera paints, paintbrushes, washcloth, tub of water, baby wipes, construction paper

Older/Younger Students
• two-four seashells, drawing paper, pencils, markers
• construction paper, clear contact paper, various colors of tissue paper, large wiggly eyes for fish

Learning Centers

(To involve children before and after Circle Time Learning)

Science Center

Option #1

Supplies Needed: seashells or plastic sea creatures, (one–three per child), a tub of water, a plastic tablecloth, and towels

1. Put the plastic tablecloth on the floor or on a table.
2. Set a tub of water with seashells/plastic sea creatures on a tablecloth.
3. Let three or four children at a time play in the water. They can add more seashells/creatures to the tub. Encourage them to compare their shells as you talk about them:

DISCUSS: Who is holding a rough shell?
Who is holding a smooth seashell?

Seashells are empty "houses" where sea animals used to live. Look inside your seashell. Can you see where a sea animal might have lived?

(hold up example) Do you know what kind of sea animal used to live in this seashell?
Doesn't God have a great imagination?
It would be hard to think up all of the different kinds of animals God created in the oceans, wouldn't it?

Who likes to eat salmon? or tuna fish?
Who likes to eat shrimp? or clams?
Who likes to eat oysters? or sardines?
They are all unique living creatures God created and put in the oceans for our enjoyment. Aren't you glad?

Let's thank God for all of them.

Science Center

Option #2

Supplies Needed: 5–8 seashells (unique and different shells), one or more sand dollars, basket or tray, cloth to cover them up

Allow the children to look at the seashells. Talk about each shell.

Explain:

1. Listen to the seashells. Put them close to your ears. Can you hear noise the ocean makes? Who lived in these shells?

2. Now let's all try to remember each shell that is here on this tray (or basket).

3. In a minute I am going to cover up all the shells with my cloth.

4. Then I will reach under the cloth and take away ONE of the shells.

5. When I show the shells to you again, see if you can figure out WHICH SHELL is missing.

6. So take a good look at all the shells and then we'll play this guessing game.

Learning Centers

Physical Center

Supplies Needed: none

Children stand in a circle around you. Choose one child to be "it."

Explain:

1. I am going to whisper the name of a sea creature in _____'s ear.

2. Then he/she will move around like that creature.

3. When you think you know what the creature is, shout it out!

4. The first one to guess the name of the creature can try it next time.

After someone guesses correctly, have ALL the children move like the sea creature named, before letting another child act out a new one.

Hint: The more involved you are in moving and having fun, the more the children will want to do it too.

Suggestions for sea creatures: shark, sea turtle, octopus, electric eel, crab, puffer fish *(puffs up)*, sword fish, whale, sting ray, seals *(bark)*, etc.

Older Children

Supplies Needed: two-three seashells, drawing paper, and pencils

1. Give children the opportunity to try to draw the seashells set out. Or let them draw their shells. *(Use pencils)*

2. Encourage children to draw as much detail as possible on their seashell.

3. At the bottom of the page, ask children to use markers to copy the words: "God made seashells. Day 5."

4. Show children how to draw the simple fish symbol some Christians put on their doors or car bumper, etc. to show they follow Jesus. I C T H U S = Jesus Christ God's Son Savior

5. Ask children if they remember when Jesus ate fish: the boy's lunch of fish and bread that fed 5,000 people (John 6:9–11), the fish Jesus ate the night after he rose from the dead (Luke 24:36–43), and the miraculous catch of fish (John 21:3–13).

Learning Centers

Art Center

Only two or three children at a time will be able to work on this. Be sure and show children a completed sample to help them understand what they need to do to make a fish print.

Supplies Needed: a whole fish or two from the local market, slightly diluted tempera paints, paintbrushes, washcloth and tub of water, construction paper, baby wipes

1. Invite one or two children at a time to paint the (washed) fish from the market.

2. Instruct them to cover the whole fish with a thin coat of paint.

3. When they finish painting, have them put their paper on top of the fish and gently rub across the whole paper/fish. Make sure not to move the paper.

4. When they have gently rubbed the whole fish, remove the paper to reveal the fish print on the bottom side of the paper.

5. Quickly wash the fish and pat dry before the next child's turn.

6. In the meantime, have children clean up with baby wipes.

Younger Children

Supplies Needed: construction paper, clear contact paper, various colors of tissue paper, large wiggly eyes

Before class:

- Cut large fish shapes from each piece of construction paper.
  Save the construction paper "frame" with the hole (after the fish is cut out).
- Cut a piece of clear contact paper the same size as the construction paper frame.
- Remove the contact paper backing. Mount contact paper on the construction paper.
  Now you have a sticky fish–shaped hole–section in the middle of your frame.
- Cut little squares (about 1.5 x 1.5") out of a variety of colored tissue papers.

During class:

1. Give each child a fish frame and a small group of tissue paper squares.

2. Show children how to push tissue paper with their finger onto the sticky fish hole to make their own brightly colored fish picture.

3. Put each child's name on his/her project and send it home.

Invite children to come to Circle Time to join you.

Circle Time Song

Review the first four verses of the "Creation Song."
Learn the fifth verse. Sing to tune of "Are You Sleeping?"

On Day one, on Day one,
God did make, God did make
Light to shine in darkness,
Light to shine in darkness.
It was good. It was good.

On Day two, on Day two,
God did make, God did make
Lots of sky and water,
Lots of sky and water.
It was good. It was good.

On Day three, on Day three,
God did make, God did make
Many trees and flowers,
Many trees and flowers.
It was good. It was good.

On Day four, on Day four,
God did make, God did make
Sun and moon and stars,
Sun and moon and stars.
It was good. It was good.

On Day five, on Day five,
God did make, God did make
All the fish and birdies,
All the fish and birdies.
It was good. It was good.

*   *   *

Other Songs:

"Everything Is Possible"
"He's Got the Whole World"

Circle Time Discussion

By now, the children should be telling you what is on the pages you already covered. Discuss what it means.

WOW! Look at all of the fish God made! But there are more creatures than just fish in this picture. What else do you see?

Why do you think God made sea creatures?

If you see what looks like a seashell with eyes, what do you think that might mean?
(A creature lives inside the shell.)

What are the largest sea creatures God made?
(The Blue Whales)

What does a crab look like? How about a jellyfish?

Would it be a good idea to go swimming with a jellyfish? How about swimming with an octopus? Why or why not?

Which kinds of sea creatures could we find in the waters around where we live?
In a river? In a pond? In a lake?

Let's take turns and each name one of our favorite sea creatures.

Why do you think God made so many different kinds of sea creatures?
(Take all answers.) God must have a lot of imagination, don't you think so?

What did God say to the sea creatures?
God "blessed them" and said, "Have little ones. Fill the water in the oceans."

The Bible says God wanted people to be in charge of all the sea creatures. How should we be in charge of all the fish and sea creatures today? *(Help keep our water clean, don't waste water, don't throw junk in rivers, lakes, and oceans, etc.)*

Should we eat these sea creatures?
In what ways can we care for them?
(Can initiate a very brief discussion here about throwing things in the water that don't belong there.)

Now let's practice our Bible Memory Verse.

Practice the Memory Verse

"God created great whales, and every living creature that moveth (moves)" (Genesis 1:21 KJV).

Practice this verse several times, then let the children take turns thinking of how to act out "every living creature that moveth (moves)." Repeat the verse each time.

EXPLAIN:
When we say "moves" (or "moveth"), I will point to one person who will show us a different way a sea creature might move. Then we will all move like that.

1. The first time through, a child might move like an octopus.

2. The second time through, a child might make a fish face with his mouth and flap his fins.

3. The third time, a child may move like an eel, and so forth. Continue to practice until everyone takes a turn, or until they recite the verse easily.

Post-Session Learning Centers

(After Circle Time, rotate children to another Learning Center)

Closing • Back to Circle Time

At the end of the class, gather the children together for a closing circle. Have the children tell what their favorite part of the day was.
Help them review each step.

Then pray together:
Thank You, God, for making so many different kinds of sea creatures for us to enjoy. Help us take good care of them.
We love You. In Jesus' Name we pray. Amen.

Next time we will learn about something else God made for us to enjoy. Can anyone guess what it is? *(Birds)*

Remember to send home Parent Page

Dear Parents,

Today: We learned a lot about fish and sea creatures. We played with seashells in water, painted real fish, pretended to move like underwater creatures, and learned that God put people in charge of all of them. Have your child sing the first five verses of the Creation Song and tell you what he or she liked best about today.

Next Time: We take to the air! God made birds on Day 5, and we want to find out about birds. This would be a good week keep track of the number and kinds of birds around your home. Leave a paper and pencil near a window. Make columns for different kinds of birds, and put tally marks every time you see a bird throughout the week.

Read: Genesis 1:20–22 with your child. When God created fish, He also made birds. Pray with your child, thanking God for His wonderful imagination in making all of the different birds. **Bring Next Time:** a feather

For Parents: Once Jesus said, ". . . Take no thought for your life . . . Look at the birds . . ." (Matthew 6:25–26). Let every little bird remind you of God's constant care for you.

Blessings to your family from our Teaching Staff

Dear Parents,

Lesson 7

Today: We learned a lot about fish and sea creatures. We played with seashells in water, painted real fish, pretended to move like underwater creatures, and learned that God put people in charge of all of them. Have your child sing the first five verses of the Creation Song and tell you what he or she liked best about today.

Next Time: We take to the air! God made birds on Day 5, and we want to find out about birds. This would be a good week keep track of the number and kinds of birds around your home. Leave a paper and pencil near a window. Make columns for different kinds of birds, and put tally marks every time you see a bird throughout the week.

Read: Genesis 1:20–22 with your child. When God created fish, He also made birds. Pray with your child, thanking God for His wonderful imagination in making all of the different birds. **Bring Next Time:** a feather

For Parents: Once Jesus said, ". . . Take no thought for your life . . . Look at the birds . . ." (Matthew 6:25–26). Let every little bird remind you of God's constant care for you.

Blessings to your family from our Teaching Staff

"God said, 'Let the waters bring forth abundantly the moving creatures'... and God created great whales... after their kind... And God blessed them, saying, Be fruitful, and multiply, and fill the waters in the sea" (Genesis 1:20-22 KJV).

Cut out and color crab. Tape or glue to a long paint stick. Hold up as you say the rhyme. Together with the children, lift up a corresponding number of your fingers on your other hand as you read the numbers in the rhyme.

Five Red Crabs

FIVE red crabs walked sideways down the shore.
One fell behind and then there were FOUR.

FOUR red crabs watched the waves of the sea.
One floated off and then there were THREE.

THREE red crabs played peek–a–boo.
One dug a hole and then there were TWO.

TWO red crabs sat resting in the sun.
One chased a sand flea and now there was ONE.

ONE red crab felt sad and all alone.
He waded in the water and swam back home.

Walk Like Crabs:

1. Sit down on the floor.
2. Stretch your arms behind you. Place hands on the floor.
3. Lean back on your hands
4. Lift your bottom off the floor (Tummy faces the ceiling).
5. "Walk" head-first on feet and hands.
6. Does anybody want to race?

SEA CREATURES

GUESS WHO I AM

In water, I'm fast; but on land, I move slooooow.

(Try hauling your house every place that you go!)

Wherever I travel, my home's on my back.

I duck quick inside at the sign of attack!

My head, all my feet, and my tail disappear.

They won't pop back out 'till the coast is all clear!

God made me to be a . . . TURTLE!

GUESS WHO I AM

The faraway North is my home — it is cold.

My whiskers and wrinkles all make me look OLD.

I dive in the ocean and swim all about.

My wet skin is slipp'ry; my two "teeth" stick out.

My flippers and tail help me walk on the ice.

Although I look grumpy, I'm really quite nice.

God made me to be a . . . WALRUS!

GUESS WHO I AM

I live in the sea, but I'm wondering why—

My name sounds the same as bright lights in the sky.

My body is strange — I have no eyes or head;

I wish I had legs — I have five arms instead!

I'm not a real fish; I can't swim, splash, or dive.

But I'm not complaining. I'm glad I'm alive!

God made me to be a . . . STAR FISH!

SEA CREATURES

GUESS WHO I AM

I live in the tide pools along the sea shore.

I'm speechless and quiet. Don't call me a bore!

Please find me a seashell that I can call "home."

I need its protection wherever I roam.

My long arms stick out on the left and the right.

With pinchers that help me when I need to fight.

God made me to be a . . . HERMIT CRAB!

GUESS WHO I AM

Propelling the water with my tail and fin,

I speed with a twist of my rubbery skin.

It's fun playing games — I am smart and I'm quick!

Just throw me a ball and I'll learn a new trick.

I leap out of water — up four feet or more.

You'll find a toy like me for sale at the store.

God made me to be a . . . DOLPHIN!

GUESS WHO I AM

I live in two shells that close shut very tight,

Protecting my delicate body at night.

By day, I peek out, then extend my small head.

But sand in my shell is one thing that I dread!

I sweep up the sand in a nice little mound,

And when I am opened, a PEARL will be found!

God made me to be an . . . OYSTER!

SEA CREATURES

GUESS WHO I AM

I love playing hide-and-go seek in the sand.

I crawl up the seashore and dig in the land.

When you're at the beach, you will find me around.

You'll have to dig fast! I move quick underground.

The shell on my body will close shut air-tight;

To guard me from harm, 'cause I'm too small to fight!

God made me to be a . . . CRAB

GUESS WHO I AM

I rest on the rocks while I bathe in the sun,

I jump in the water — let's play and have fun!

My smooth, slippery body speeds fast in the sea;

On land I move slower (I've no legs on me).

When I get excited, you'll hear my loud BARK.

I yelp to warn others when I spot a shark!

God made me to be a . . . SEAL!

GUESS WHO I AM

Beware when you see my fin glide through the sea,

Please head for the shore when you see that it's me.

Men scream when they see me — I'm scary indeed!

I quickly attack with my lightning-fast speed.

I thrash in the water when grabbing my food,

Or when I feel mad or am in a bad mood.

God made me to be a . . . SHARK!

SEA CREATURES

GUESS WHO I AM

Sea caves or old ship wrecks make me a fine home.

I swim and I slither quite fast when I roam.

I lack arms or hands; I'm without legs or feet.

Sharp teeth and strong jaws help me catch what I eat;

My bite is electric, alarming my prey.

You'd best keep your distance when you're in my way!

God made me to be an . . . ELECTRIC EEL!

GUESS WHO I AM

I'm hungry! I need lots of food for my snacks.

My mouth opens wide — I eat fish by the stacks!

I lunge through the sea, making waves like a storm;

My layers of fat keep me heated and warm.

My blow-spout breathes air from a hole in my back.

Although I look fierce, I don't often attack!

God made me to be a . . . WHALE!

GUESS WHO I AM

I hide among caves in the ocean so deep.

I'm quite shy and noiseless — I don't make a peep.

My big wrinkled head looks for crabs I can eat;

Eight arms catch my food — I have no hands or feet!

When I am afraid of a shark chasing me,

I squirt out black ink so that it cannot see!

God made me to be an . . . OCTOPUS!

God Creates BIRDS

"And God created. . . every winged fowl after his kind: and God saw that it was good. And God blessed them, saying, Be fruitful, and multiply, and. . . let fowl multiply in the earth" (Genesis 1:20, 22 KJV).

Get Ready:

☐ **PRAY** throughout the week that God will bless you and your children with understanding of the awesome power of His creation.

☐ **MAKE COPIES** of the parent take-home page (for a group class).

☐ **CONTACT ASSISTANTS** Go over the things you would like them to do in class.

☐ **PREPARE** pre–cut shapes needed for the art project. Write the memory verse on the bottom of each piece of construction paper.

☐ **GATHER** *The Creation Story for Children* (optional) plus other materials for your centers and circle time.

Welcome parents and children as they arrive.
Remember to call each one by name.
Invite children to join one of the learning centers.

Learning Center Supplies

Physical Center
#1 – none
#2 – a book with pictures of various kinds of birds

Science Center
#1 – feathers
#2 – a flat pan with a variety of birdseed, magnifying glasses, tweezers, muffin tin *(Note: You can buy a bag of birdseed at a pet store or variety store.)*

Art Center
#1 – precut shapes (circles, ovals, triangles), glue sticks, construction paper, feathers, birdseed
#2 – construction paper, crayons, scissors, glue

Older/Younger Students
• straw, mud, small sticks, string, and paper bowls
• a bowl, a raw egg, and several boiled eggs

Learning Centers

(To involve children before and after Circle Time Learning)

Physical Center

Option #1

Supplies Needed: *none*
Have children stand in a circle around you.

Explain: Today we are going to pretend to be birds. When I call out an activity, you act out what a bird would do.

For example, if I call out "FLYING," you will spread your wings and fly around the circle. If I call out "BATHING," you pretend to be in a puddle or birdbath splashing water on your wings.

If I call out "SLEEPING," put your head under your "wing" to sleep. If I call out "EATING," you will pull a nice, fat, juicy worm out of the ground and chew it.

NOTE: Practice each of the motions, then tell a story of a day in the life of a bird.

When you get to an action item, say it in a louder voice so children don't miss it. *(Hint: The more you are animated and the more fun you have, the more the children will imitate you.)*

For example: "Once upon a time, there was a little bird named Feathers. One day when Feathers WOKE UP, he FLEW down by the river and took a BATH. He SPLASHED cold water all over his body.

Then he WALKED around in the grass, LOOKING for breakfast. He PULLED a fat worm out of the ground. While he was EATING the fat juicy worm, his mother FLEW down beside him. 'Feathers, did you remember to THANK God for your breakfast?' she asked. . . . "

Continue with a story about Feathers. Let the children help decide what actions come next.

Physical Center

Option #2

Supplies Needed: *a book with pictures of various kinds of birds*

1. Give each child a turn to name one specific kind of bird God made.

2. Let the child also decide how that kind of bird might use its wings. Have the child demonstrate wing motions.

3. Invite all the other children to imitate the motions of how each bird that is named uses its wings.

EXAMPLES:

- An eagle spreads its huge wings and glides through the sky. *(Stretch arms out as wide as possible.)*
- A hummingbird's tiny wings always move faster than any other bird. *(Rapidly flap only your hands.)*
- An ostrich's wings flutter at its side while it runs *(Flutter arms at side, run in place).*
- Robins and other birds with short wings flap wings as they fly *(Flap only forearms and hands).*
- A penguin's wings hang down at its side as it waddles. Its wings also help glide through the water.
- A woodpecker's wings fold tightly at its side when it pecks on a tree trunk, looking for food.

Learning Centers

Science Center

Option #1

Supplies Needed: an assortment of feathers

- Invite the children to show their feathers. *(Explain where they found the feathers.)*
- Touch and compare feathers. See how light they feel.
- Examine feathers under a magnifying glass.

Discuss:

Which feathers are black? . . . blue? . . . red?
Which feathers have more than one color?
Which feather is your favorite? Why?
Which feathers did you *(or "would you")* find in your yard? . . . in the park? . . . under a tree?
Wonder out loud what kind of birds might have dropped each of the feathers.

Option #2

Supplies Needed: a flat pan with a variety of birdseed in it, magnifying glasses (muffin tin and tweezers to help sort seeds)

Let students examine different kinds of birdseed with a magnifying glass.

Do you know what these seeds are?
Do we ever eat any of these seeds?
Where do the seeds come from?
(From plants God made: wheat, millet, barley, etc.)

What should we do with all the seeds when we finish looking at them?

Note: To extend this activity, add muffin tins and tweezers. Let older children use tweezers to pick up the seeds and sort them into the muffin tins.

Older Children

Supplies Needed: straw, mud, small sticks, string, and paper bowls
(Show pictures so children can get some ideas of what nests look like)

God made all the birds and gave them the ability to make amazing nests.
How easy do you think it would be to build a bird's nest? Do you want to try?
Birds must build their nests to be very strong. Do you know WHY?

(So a bad stormy wind or heavy rain won't blow them fall apart. So the nests are sturdy enough to hold a bunch of eggs and also to hold the baby birds as they grow, etc.)

Here are some supplies. How would you start building a nest?
Each of you take one bowl. See if you can build a sturdy nest that will last.
Make the nest any way you would like. Do you need anything else?

*NOTE: Give children a chance to figure out how they want to make their nest.
This is much harder than it looks at first. Allow the nests (with mud) to dry. (Send home in a sack.)
Have the children report back later on whether or not their nest held together.*

Learning Centers

Art Center

Option #1

This craft project can be done as a large–group exercise or as a Center activity.

Supplies Needed: precut shapes (circles, ovals, triangles), construction paper, and glue sticks (Can decorate with feathers or birdseed)

(Idea of what your birds might look like.)

Option #2

Supplies Needed: construction paper, glue, crayons, scissors (can also include feathers and/or birdseed)

Set out materials. Allow children to use their imaginations to make pictures.

These are usually less recognizable than the crafts, but they allow children to practice using their own imaginations and problem-solving skills.

Younger Children

Supplies Needed: a bowl, a raw egg (or two), and several boiled eggs

Gather 3-5 children around you.

Discuss:

- Have you ever looked inside an egg? Maybe you've helped someone while they were cooking. Have you seen the insides of an egg before it was cooked? Let's look!

- Crack the raw egg into the bowl. Allow children to take turns looking in the bowl. Discuss: What do you see? *As the children respond, talk to them about each part of the egg.*

- The yellow yolk is the food God put inside the egg so the baby bird will be able to grow strong. The clear, kind of slimy part will grow to be a baby bird. The clear, kind of runny part is to keep the baby bird from hurting itself on the egg shell before it is hatched.

- Now let's look inside a cooked egg. Can you find the yolk? Can you find the clear part? It turned white, didn't it?

Explain: We don't eat eggs that are raw, or that haven't been cooked. *(Slice the boiled eggs to give everyone a taste.)*

- Isn't it amazing how God put all those neat things inside a little egg? I wonder how God did it. God can do a lot of wonderful things people can't do!

Invite children to come to Circle Time to join you.

Circle Time Song

Review first five verses of the "Creation Song."
Sing to the tune of "Frere Jacques" ("Are You Sleeping?").

On Day one, on Day one,
God did make, God did make
Light to shine in darkness,
Light to shine in darkness.
It was good. It was good.

On Day two, on Day two,
God did make, God did make
Lots of sky and water,
Lots of sky and water.
It was good. It was good.

On Day three, on Day three,
God did make, God did make
Many trees and flowers,
Many trees and flowers.
It was good. It was good.

On Day four, on Day four,
God did make, God did make
Sun and moon and stars,
Sun and moon and stars.
It was good. It was good.

On Day five, on Day five,
God did make, God did make
All the fish and birdies,
All the fish and birdies.
It was good. It was good.

* * *

Other Songs:

"Everything Is Possible"
"He's Got the Whole World"
"God Is So Good"

Circle Time Discussion

Do you know what God created on the same day the fish were created? *(Birds)*

Now look at all the different kinds of birds on this page! All birds have wings, feathers, and a beak. Can you find some wings, feathers, or beaks? *(Help them look)*

Do you know the names of some of these birds? *(Let children take turns pointing out different birds whose names they know.)*

Who can find a turkey? a rooster? a duck? a peacock? an eagle? a seagull? What other birds do you know?

Do you know some of these birds are as tall as grown–ups? *(Ostrich, emu)*

Most birds can fly, but do you know which birds are so heavy they can't fly? *(A penguin, an emu, and an ostrich)*

Do you know which is the smallest bird? *(Hummingbird)* Which birds are colorful? *(Point out parrots, flamingos, peacocks, etc.)*

What birds have only white and brown feathers? *(Point out the eagle and the hawk)*

Which kinds of birds live in our town? Why do you think God made so many kinds of birds? *(God gives us all things to enjoy.)*

Different kinds of birds do well in different places and climates. For example, woodpeckers like to live around wood or trees. Ducks like lots of water. Penguins like snow and ice. Parrots like hot jungles.

What does a duck need? *(Ponds, rivers, or lakes)* Where do eagles like to build nests? *(On high rocks)*

Could people have made all these different kinds of birds? No! Only God can make birds. What did God say about the birds? *(They were "good.")*

Are even vultures good? Yes, God gave the vultures a job to do. They help clean up the earth. All the birds have a place in our big world and we get to enjoy them all!

Now let's practice our Bible Memory Verse.

Practice the Memory Verse

"And God created. . . every winged fowl after his kind" (Genesis 1:21 KJV).

This is a short verse, so the children should pick it up quickly.

Have them repeat the verse as they "flap their wings."
(Show them how to put their thumbs in their armpits and move their elbows up and down.)

Continue to practice until children seem confident in saying the verse.

Post-Session Learning Centers

(After Circle Time, rotate children to another Learning Center)

Closing • Back to Circle Time

At the end of the class, gather the children together for a closing circle.
Have the children tell what their favorite part of the day was.
Help them review each step.

Then pray together:
**Thank You, God, for making so many different kinds of birds.
Thank You for making them sing so beautifully. Thank You for
making so many things for us to enjoy! In Jesus' Name. Amen**

Next week we will learn about something else God made for us
to enjoy. Can anyone guess what it is? *(Animals)*

Remember to send home Parent Page

Dear Parents,

Today: We talked about many of the birds that God made. We compared the feathers we brought in, pretended to fly, made up a story about birds, made bird pictures, looked at eggs, and marveled at God's creativity. Have your child sing the first five verses of the Creation Song to you. Let your child tell you what he/she liked best about today.

Next Time: We have a lot of creatures to study! Not only has God made a wonderful variety of fish and birds, but the million+ species of the animal world are amazing in their diversity! Can you and your child name one animal for every letter of the alphabet? *(For "x" put the letter at the end of the word—fox.)*

Read: Genesis 1:24–25 with your child. Discuss what is meant by "beasts" (or "livestock"). What creatures crawl on the ground? What is your favorite animal? What is your child's favorite animal? Why?

Bring Next Time: a favorite stuffed animal

For Parents: Many people consider humans to be in the same category as the animals God made. But no animals were made in the "image" of God. Thank God for making human beings with unique abilities to communicate, to imagine, to create, to problem-solve, to praise God . . . and to laugh! :)

Blessings to your family from our Teaching Staff

Dear Parents,

Lesson 8

Today: We talked about many of the birds that God made. We compared the feathers we brought in, pretended to fly, made up a story about birds, made bird pictures, looked at eggs, and marveled at God's creativity. Have your child sing the first five verses of the Creation Song to you. Let your child tell you what he/she liked best about today.

Next Time: We have a lot of creatures to study! Not only has God made a wonderful variety of fish and birds, but the million+ species of the animal world are amazing in their diversity! Can you and your child name one animal for every letter of the alphabet? *(For "x" put the letter at the end of the word—fox.)*

Read: Genesis 1:24–25 with your child. Discuss what is meant by "beasts" (or "livestock"). What creatures crawl on the ground? What is your favorite animal? What is your child's favorite animal? Why?

Bring Next Time: a favorite stuffed animal

For Parents: Many people consider humans to be in the same category as the animals God made. But no animals were made in the "image" of God. Thank God for making human beings with unique abilities to communicate, to imagine, to create, to problem-solve, to praise God . . . and to laugh! :)

Blessings to your family from our Teaching Staff

God Creates BIRDS

"And God created… every winged fowl after his kind: and God saw that it was good. And God blessed them, saying, Be fruitful, and multiply, and… let fowl multiply in the earth" (Genesis 1:20, 22 KJV).

Five Little Birds

FIVE brave birds flew down to the shore.
One got lost and then there were FOUR.

FOUR happy birds perched high in a tree.
One flew away and then there were THREE.

THREE hungry birds wondered what to do.
One chased a bug and then there were TWO.

TWO chirping birds sang loudly in the sun.
One hopped away and now there was ONE.

ONE sad bird on the branch all alone;
He flapped his little wings
and flew back home.

Give each child a set
of five circle birds to
color and cut out.
Glue each bird on
a flat wooden stick.
Have children hold up the right
number of birds
while the rhyme is read.

Birds

GUESS WHO I AM

I swing on my perch as I talk and tell jokes.
My colorful feathers attract many folks.
God taught me to mimic the sounds that I hear.
Oh, how I love talking to birds in my mirror!
I crack open nuts with my powerful beak.
Please don't interrupt when I'm trying to speak!
God made me to be a . . . PARROT!

GUESS WHO I AM

I'm the biggest of birds, too heavy to fly.
I lay my huge egg on the ground where it's dry.
My egg is so tough that it won't even crack,
If five kids your size climbed up onto its back.
My feet with two toes swiftly race o'er the land.
You'll laugh when I "hide" with my head in the sand!
God made me to be an . . . OSTRICH!

GUESS WHO I AM

You'll find me on coastlines and beaches of sand.
I dive in the water. I scavenge on land.
And early each morning, I forage the shore,
To peck at sand dollars, fleas, and much more.
When visitors come to explore on the beach,
I fly high above them and make a loud screech.
God made me to be a . . . SEAGULL!

Birds

GUESS WHO I AM

God made me the smallest of all birds that fly.

My wings beat the fastest. I'm not sure just why.

Up, sideways, and backwards, I fly through the trees.

My wings help me hover, even when there's a breeze.

My nest is the size of a walnut—it's small!

I have the most beautiful feathers of all.

God made me to be a . . . HUMMINGBIRD!

GUESS WHO I AM

When I started growing, an egg was my home.

God gave me two wings, but I never have flown.

I love icy water! I jump in so bold!

I dive in and splash, even though it's quite cold,

My black and white outfit looks just like a suit.

I'm dressed neat and fancy. Oh, don't I look CUTE?

God made me to be a . . . PENGUIN!

GUESS WHO I AM

My feathers are white from my head to my toe.

My long neck and body gleam white as the snow.

Folks take out their cameras where they see me glide;

They all take my picture along the lakeside.

My chicks like to ride on my back when they're small.

Compared to large birds, I'm more graceful than all!

God made me to be a . . . SWAN!

God Creates ANIMALS

"God said, 'Let the earth bring forth the living creature after his kind, cattle, and creeping thing, and beast of the earth after his kind: and it was so" (Genesis 1:24 KJV).

Welcome parents and children as they arrive. Remember to call each one by name. Invite children to join one of the learning centers.

Get Ready:

☐ **PRAY** throughout the week that God will bless you and your children with understanding of the awesome power of His creation.

☐ **MAKE COPIES** of the parent take-home page (for a group class).

☐ **CONTACT ASSISTANTS** Go over the things you would like them to do in class.

☐ **PREPARE** Set up three areas. One for wild animals, one for livestock, and one for animals that move along the ground. Put library books in the appropriate areas.

If worms are not readily available in your yard, you can find them at a bait shop with fishing gear.

☐ **GATHER** *The Creation Story for Children* (optional) plus other materials for your centers and circle time.

Learning Center Supplies

Physical Center
#1 – an assortment of stuffed animals or pictures of animals or library books of animals
#2 – none

Science Center
a plastic tub with some dirt in it, cornmeal, and four or five worms, black and white construction paper, a flashlight

Art Center
construction paper, magazines for cutting, one pair of scissors for each child, glue sticks

Older/Younger Students
• books from the library about different animals
• books with pictures of animals

Learning Centers

(To involve children before and after Circle Time Learning)

Physical Center

Option #1

Supplies Needed: give each child a stuffed animal or picture of animals of all kinds (out of magazines or books)

Explain:

This is a game for your animals.

I am going to call out different animals.

If I call "wild animals" and you are holding a wild animal, then you can make the noise your animal makes. You can move around the circle the way your animal moves.

Let's practice. If I am holding a monkey, will I go when "livestock" is called? No.

Will I go with the animals that "crawl on the ground"?
No.
Will I go when wild animals or "beasts" are called? Yes!

Demonstrate: Go around the circle moving and sounding like a monkey.

NOTE: If you have a lot of fun with this, the children will too. Begin the game in earnest when most of the children seem to understand the idea.

Physical Center

Option #2
Guessing Game

1. Extend first option: Let children take turns calling an animal's name.
2. Then have all the children move around the room like that animal.

3. **Ask questions** about the animal: **"Do worms make a noise?" "Do worms run?"**

4. Extend the activity by giving one child a chance to think of an animal and then give CLUES so the other children can guess.

Give a few examples to help children understand what to do..

I am thinking of an animal that lives in the forest (*pause*)**. It has four short, strong legs and a short white tail** (*pause*)**. It also has two long ears and a pink nose** (*pause*)**. It moves by hopping from place to place.**

1. When someone guesses RABBIT, all of the children can hop across the room and back. Teacher can give one or two more examples before giving the children a turn to think of an animal.
2. When you think they are ready, ask:
   Has anyone else got some clues about another animal we can guess?

   (Continue as long as interest and time allow.)

Learning Centers

Science Center

Supplies Needed: a plastic tub with dirt in it, four or five worms, cornmeal, black and white construction paper, a flashlight (NOTE: Worms like to eat cornmeal, so if you want to leave this Center out more than an hour, the cornmeal will be important.)

- Have four or five children at a time join you at the science table.

- Give each child a piece of white construction paper and a piece of black construction paper.

- Lay papers down touching each other.

- Place a worm on the papers with half of its body on the black paper and half on the white paper.

- Shine the flashlight on the white side and watch the worms to see what they do. Let children take turns with flashlight.

Ask the children:

What do you notice about the worms? *(They don't have eyes or ears that we can see and no arms or legs. They squirm a lot. They can crawl in any direction using either end of their body, etc.)*

What are the worms doing on the black and white papers? What does this mean?

Do worms seem to like the dark better, or do they like the light better? How do you know they like the dark better?

(Be sure the children treat the worms gently. Let each child who wants a turn have one.)

Older Children

Supplies Needed: some books about animals if you have them

Play a guessing game or use *"Who Am I?" CREATURE CLUES* in this book.

Which land animal did God make the tallest of all? *(Giraffe)*
Which is the biggest animal God made on the land? *(Elephant)*
Which animal carries its babies in a pouch? *(Kangaroo)*
Which animal smells with its tongue? *(Snake)*
Which animals have no legs or arms? *(Worms, snakes)*
Which animal runs the fastest *(Cheetah - 46 mph)*
Which animal has sharp, prickly quills? *(Porcupine)*
Which animal gives off a terrible smell? *(Skunk)*
Which animal can go a long time without food or water? *(Camel)*
Which animal has a thick fur coat to keep it warm in the coldest places? *(Polar bears)*
Which animal gives us a lot of good food to eat? *(Cow—milk, cheese, ice cream, yogurt, butter)*

NOTE: Involve all the children. Give students an opportunity to make up their own quiz questions for classmates.

Learning Centers

Art Center

NOTE: This art project can be done as a large group exercise or as a Center activity.

Supplies Needed: construction paper, magazines for cutting, scissors, glue sticks. Give each child his or her own magazine and scissors.

Explain:
Today we are going to see how many animals you can find in these pages.

1. Look through your magazine and cut out all of the animals you find. It doesn't matter if they are "beasts," livestock, or wild animals, or animals that crawl along the ground. If you find two of the same animals, give one to another child so he or she can add it to his or her paper.

2. After you cut out a picture, glue it on your paper to take home.

3. If you fill up one side of your paper, you can start on the back.

4. Let's take turns with show and tell. First show your paper. Then tell everyone what animal(s) you have glued on your paper. I'm so glad God made lots of great animals!

Younger Children

Supplies Needed: pictures of a variety of animals

1. Gather three or four children together.

2. Allow each of them to choose a picture of one animal that God made.

3. Take turns asking each child if they know how that animal might move. Give suggestions if the child need help.

4. Ask all children to move like the animal. Discuss how it feels to move like this.

What would it be like to move like this all the time? Why is it good for a (lion) **to** (move slowly through the grass), **or a** (duck) **to** (waddle to the water), **etc.?**
I'm so glad God made (giraffes) **and** (funny monkeys!). **It's fun to walk like a** (gorilla)."
NOTE: Allow children to stay as long as interest holds. Usually young children will participate in this kind of activity for a short while, leave to check out what else is going on, and then come back.

Invite children to come to Circle Time to join you.

Circle Time Song

Review the first five verses of the "Creation Song."
Teach verse 6.
Sing to the tune of "Frere Jacques" ("Are You Sleeping?").

On Day one, on Day one,
God did make, God did make
Light to shine in darkness,
Light to shine in darkness.
It was good. It was good.

On Day two, on Day two,
God did make, God did make
Lots of sky and water,
Lots of sky and water.
It was good. It was good.

On Day three, on Day three,
God did make, God did make
Many trees and flowers,
Many trees and flowers.
It was good. It was good.

On Day four, on Day four,
God did make, God did make
Sun and moon and stars,
Sun and moon and stars.
It was good. It was good.

On Day five, on Day five,
God did make, God did make
All the fish and birdies,
All the fish and birdies.
It was good. It was good.

On Day six, on Day six,
God did make, God did make
All the other animals,
All the other animals.
God made man, woman too.

* * *

Other Songs:

"Everything Is Possible"

"God Is So Good"

"He's Got the Whole World"

Circle Time Discussion

What does it mean when the Bible says God made "beasts" (or "livestock" — NIrV)? What are "beasts"? *(Big, strong animals)* Can anyone tell me one animal that might be considered livestock? Anyone else?

Where are some animals that crawl on the ground? *(Snakes, reptiles, and amphibians all fall into this category.)*

Are all of these animals safe for us to pet? No. All these animals, even the cute ones, can hurt us if we don't know how to hold them or pet them. Leave them alone unless your mom or dad tells you it is okay.

Every one of these animals is really good at something. Maybe God made so many different animals because God wanted to give examples of good things we also can do.

Which animal do you think is the strongest? *(Elephant)* Which animal is the tallest? *(Giraffe)* Which animal can walk the longest without stopping for a drink? *(Camel)*

What animals are good at protecting themselves from other animals who would try to eat them? *(Skunk, armadillo. porcupine)*

Can you think of other things a particular animal is good at? *(Examples: best sight, best hearing, longest teeth, loudest roar, longest tongue, best hand–washer, best runner, etc.)*

How are WE different from animals? *(We can pray to God. We can love each other, laugh, think big thoughts, and make lots of things. We are special!)*

God made ALL creatures good at something! Some of us are good at singing or playing instruments. Some of us are good helpers. Some are good runners or jumpers. What is something you are good at? Some of us are also good at learning!

So now let's practice our Bible Memory Verse.

Practice the Memory Verse

God said, "Let the earth bring forth the living creature after his kind" (Genesis 1:24 KJV).

- Have the children stand in a circle around you.

- Ask children to put their stuffed animals in the center of the circle.

- Practice the memory verse as you walk around the circle and look at all of the kinds of animals the children brought.

- The second time through, reverse direction of your walk.

- Continue in this manner until the children have memorized the verse.

Post-Session Learning Centers

(After Circle Time, rotate children to another Learning Center)

Closing • Back to Circle Time

At the end of the class, gather the children together for a closing circle.
Have the children **tell** what their favorite part of the day was. Help them **review** each step.

Then pray together:

Thank You, God, for making so many different kinds of animals. Thank You for making them each good at something. Thank You for making each of us good at something! In Jesus' Name. Amen.

There is one more thing God made we haven't talked about yet.

Can anyone guess what it is? *(When God made a man and a woman.)*

Remember to send home Parent Page

Dear Parents,

Today: We studied the huge number of different kinds of animals God made. We sorted them into different categories, imitated them, and discovered each animal is good at something. Ask your child to sing the Creation Song and tell you what his or her favorite part of the day was.

Next Time: We will find out what God made before He rested. God made man and woman! We are God's special creation, made in God's image. Spend some time this week noticing many of the wonderful things God designed about our bodies. For example, all of our senses make our lives more exciting. God gave us an imagination and lots of creativity to serve Him.

Read: Genesis 1:26–31 with your child. Help your child be thankful for the gift of his or her body.

Things to Bring Next Time: a favorite boy or girl doll

For Parents: What does that mean to you that you have been created in God's image? How do you view yourself? Do you only see what you *can't* do or *don't* have? Take time to reflect on the great gifts God has given you in your body. Thank God for all you have and are and do.

Blessings to your family from our Teaching Staff

Dear Parents,

Lesson 9

Today: We studied the huge number of different kinds of animals God made. We sorted them into different categories, imitated them, and discovered each animal is good at something. Ask your child to sing the Creation Song and tell you what his or her favorite part of the day was.

Next Time: We will find out what God made before He rested. God made man and woman! We are God's special creation, made in God's image. Spend some time this week noticing many of the wonderful things God designed about our bodies. For example, all of our senses make our lives more exciting. God gave us an imagination and lots of creativity to serve Him.

Read: Genesis 1:26–31 with your child. Help your child be thankful for the gift of his or her body.

Things to Bring Next Time: a favorite boy or girl doll

For Parents: What does that mean to you that you have been created in God's image? How do you view yourself? Do you only see what you *can't* do or *don't* have? Take time to reflect on the great gifts God has given you in your body. Thank God for all you have and are and do.

Blessings to your family from our Teaching Staff

"God said, 'Let the earth bring forth the living creature after his kind, cattle, and creeping thing, and beast of the earth after his kind: and it was so" (Genesis 1:24 KJV).

Extra Game & Discussion:

Game: Animal Sounds

1. Have everyone sit in a circle with one child in the center. Ask the child in the center to think of an animal or bird without saying what he has chosen.

2. The child then asks another child in the circle: "What sound does a _____*(whatever animal he has chosen)* make?"

3. The child who was asked must try to make the sound of that particular animal.

4. The child who makes the correct sound gets to sit in the center and ask the same question of the group, using the name of another animal or bird of his choice.

Discussion Questions:

• Which animal is your favorite? Why?

• If you could have any animal in the world as a pet, which would you select? Why?

• Can you think of some animals who show us God's sense of humor?

• What animal do you think is the funniest?

• What animal is the slowest? . . . the quietest? . . . loudest ? . . . most colorful? . . . furriest?. . smartest? . . . cutest? . . . prickliest? . . . smelliest? . . . most beautiful? . . . most intelligent?

• What about YOU and ME ? How are PEOPLE different from animals? *(We can talk to God. We can smile and laugh. We can talk to each other a LOT. No other animal uses its imagination to make things and be creative like we can.)*

We can clearly see that PEOPLE are a very special creation of God.
THANK YOU , GOD, FOR MAKING LOTS OF ANIMALS . . . and for making us!

Garden Creatures

Introduction

God made lots of insects with three pairs of legs;
Three parts to our bodies; we all hatch from eggs.
God gave every insect a shape and a size.
The beetle and ladybug; earthworm and flies.
Think hard. Listen closely. Try guessing and see.
You'll find us in gardens. Oh, WHO can we be?
God made some of us . . . INSECTS!

GUESS WHO I AM

When you have a picnic, you'd better watch out!
We crawl in your cookies and bread strewn about.
We'll carry big crumbs of your food on our back,
To share with our friends for an afternoon snack.
Although we're quite tiny, we work very hard.
You'll find us quite busy in your house or yard!
God made us to be . . . ANTS!

GUESS WHO I AM

Most people don't like me. They call me a "pest!"
They chase me and swat me. I don't get much rest.
My specialized feet help me hang upside down.
When you hear me buzzing, don't swat me or frown.
Frogs catch me and eat me for dinner or snack.
If your mama sees me, she'll give me a WHACK!
God made me to be a . . . FLY!

Garden Creatures

GUESS WHO I AM

Peek under a plant in a small secret space;

A log or dead leaf is our great hiding place.

Our pinchers look scary; our faces look mean.

We won't actually *bite* you; we keep your yard clean.

Black pinchers and horns give our enemies fright;

But you'll enjoy some of us glowing at night!

God made us to be . . . BEETLES!

GUESS WHO I AM

Have you seen me jump with my strong six black legs?

I hop, leap, and crawl. I lay many small eggs.

I sing quiet tunes in the darkness of night,

By rubbing my legs close together just right.

I have a black shell on my back, tough and hard.

Come listen! I'll chirp you a song in your yard!

God made me to be a . . . CRICKET!

GUESS WHO I AM

God taught me to spin a web structure of art.

When you see my "strings," please don't pull them apart.

In small shapes and sizes, I spin and I weave

To catch tasty dinners I later retrieve.

My eight skinny legs help me move quick and fast.

Hooray! I've caught a fly in my webbing at last!

God made me to be a . . . SPIDER!

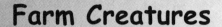

Farm Creatures

GUESS WHO I AM

My nose sniffs and twitches—*(that* gives you a clue).

My four furry feet run much faster than you.

I dash, hop, and zigzag all over the ground.

My long, floppy ears hear the quietest sound.

God gave me a tail, very fluffy and white.

My teeth chew up veggies in gardens at night.

God made me to be a . . . RABBIT!

GUESS WHO I AM

I'm cute and I'm cuddly with fluffy, soft fur.

Whenever I'm happy, I make a sweet *purr.*

I'll pounce on your bed with my soft, fuzzy paws.

Watch out! I might scratch you with sharp, pointed claws.

I like to climb trees. I love playing with yarn,

And sometimes I chase after mice in the barn.

God made me to be a . . . KITTEN!

GUESS WHO I AM

God gave me short whiskers, four feet, and a tail.

I'm a small, quiet pet; some stores have me for sale.

Girls scream when they see me! They jump on a chair!

I dash through the kitchen and give them a *scare.*

I love to eat cheese, but I **don't** like your cat!

If you see me running, don't call me a *rat*

God made me to be a . . . MOUSE!

Farm Creatures

GUESS WHO I AM

My warm, woolly coat, like a white puffy cloud,

Will make you some clothes — and of that I am proud!

I love grassy hills where I wander and roam.

Sometimes I get lost and can't find my way home.

I'm easily frightened, quite timid, and shy.

And if something scares me, you'll hear my "baaaaa" cry.

God made me to be a . . . LAMB!

GUESS WHO I AM

You'll find me in meadows. I eat grass and hay.

I sleep in a barn at the end of the day.

Each morning I give out my world-renowned drink.

It starts off your day the best way, don't you think?

Without me, you'd never eat ice cream or cheese.

When you want my specialties, always say PLEASE!

God made me to be a . . . COW!

GUESS WHO I AM

I roll in mud puddles; I like how mud feels.

I eat kitchen scraps — piles of smelly mush mounds.

Oh, how I love mud! Hear my grunts, oinks, and squeals.

I slurp when I eat, making loud, silly sounds!

I'm round with a pink curly tail. I am FAT.

But everyone tells me they like me like that

God made me to be a . . . PIG!

Zoo Creatures

GUESS WHO I AM

I live in Australia, high up in a tree.

A lot of stuffed animals look just like me.

I'm everyone's favorite, so cuddly and cute,

With furry round ears and a soft fuzzy suit.

I'm friendly to all. I have no enemies.

I'm peaceful and kind—like God wants us to be.

God made me to be a . . . KOALA BEAR!

GUESS WHO I AM

Through trees in the jungle, I scamper and swing.

I screech, scream, and holler. I wish I could sing!

My long tail and arms help me climb up the trees

To play with my cousins, the fun chimpanzees.

In many big cities, I live at the zoo.

Please come there and watch me. I'd like to watch YOU!

God made me to be a . . . MONKEY!

GUESS WHO I AM

Of mothers who care for their kids, I'm the best!

God gave me a "nest" quite unique from the rest.

I carry my baby up front in a pouch,

It's cozy and soft, like your living room couch.

My baby can climb out to wander and play,

Or hop out and follow me during the day.

God made me to be a . . . KANGAROO!

Zoo Creatures

GUESS WHO I AM

I'm king of the jungle. Please call me by name.

I'm wild and ferocious! I'll never be tame!

My frightening roar can be heard far and wide.

When animals hear me, they feel terrified!

Sometimes kids call me a "big pussycat,"

But I'm not so friendly. You won't want to "chat"!

God made me to be a . . . LION!

GUESS WHO I AM

I smell very well with my extra-long nose.

And sometimes I squirt with it—just like a hose.

God covered me over with gray wrinkled skin—

It's saggy and baggy, to my great chagrin!

I use my big ears like a fan when I'm hot.

If flies buzz and bother, my tail gives a SWAT!

God made me to be an . . . ELEPHANT!

GUESS WHO I AM

I like to roam free on the African plain.

I'm covered with stripes from my tail to my mane.

You'll find me with friends, sticking close to our "herd."

Our black and white patterns, some think are absurd.

I look very much like a donkey or horse,

But I'm more dressed up and more handsome, of course!

God made me to be a . . . ZEBRA!

God Creates PEOPLE

"The Lord God formed man of the dust of the ground, and breathed into his nostrils the breath of life; and man became a living soul... And the Lord God... made he a woman, and brought her unto the man" (Genesis 2:7, 22 KJV).

Get Ready:

☐ **PRAY** throughout the week that God will bless you and your children with understanding of the awesome power of His creation.

☐ **MAKE COPIES** of the parent take-home page.

☐ **CONTACT ASSISTANTS** to remind them that you look forward to working with them. Go over the things you would like them to do in class.

☐ **PREPARE** for Science Center a large graph on which to place square-sized boys and square-sized girls. Also prepare a dramatic play area where children can play with dolls. Include a kitchen set, dishes, and dress-up clothes.

☐ **GATHER** *The Creation Story for Children* (optional) plus other materials for your centers and circle time.

Welcome parents and children as they arrive. Remember to call each one by name if you can. Invite children to join one of the learning centers.

Learning Center Supplies

Physical Center
#1 – blindfolds *(cloth hair bands work well)*
#2 – none

Science Center
dolls, plus small pictures of boys and girls, a large graph with squares on which to put the pictures, scotch tape, knife, jelly beans in clear glass jar

Art Center
small, plain paper plates or circles of various skin tones, markers, yarn, glue sticks, mirrors, plus the *CREATION Big Book* page with picture of earth and many children's faces

Older/Younger Students
• none
• dolls, props for playing house

Learning Centers

(To involve children before and after Circle Time Learning)

Physical Center

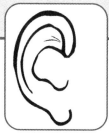

Option #1

Supplies Needed: blindfolds (cloth hair bands work well for blindfolds)

Explain: Our EARS are wonderful gifts God made. God gave us two ears. Ears help us learn things by hearing and listening.

For example, if I couldn't see where you were, I could listen very carefully and find out where you were.

Demonstrate: Blindfold yourself. Ask a child to move around and say, "Hello."

Now you try it. I will give each of you a hair band to cover your eyes. Then I will move around the room and you will try to find me. Your trick is you have to find me . . . without looking! You won't be able to see with your eyes. You will have to use your EARS to find me.

(Some of the more timid children may want to blindfold their dolls instead.)

My trick is that every five seconds, I will say "Jesus loves me." So listen very carefully if you want to find out where I am!

NOTE: Continue game until time is up or for as long as interest holds.

Physical Center

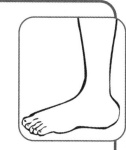

Option #2

Supplies Needed: none

<u>Explain</u> the game of SIMON SAYS: God made our bodies to be able to do a lot of great things. I will think of something, then I'll do it and tell you to do it too. But you should only do it if I <u>first</u> say, "Simon says."

Let's practice:

1. God made me to run in place.
   Simon says, "Run in place." (run)

2. God made my elbows to bend.
   Simon says, "Bend your elbows."

3. God made my eyes to blink.
   Simon says, "Blink your eyes."

4. Try more items *(wave hands, wiggle fingers, etc.)*, and then the next time leave out "Simon says."

Remind children not to move unless they first hear the words: "Simon says."

Once they understand the game, children will want to be "Simon." Let children take turns leading until time runs out. Finish by thanking God for our wonderful bodies and all we can do.

Learning Centers

Science Center

Supplies Needed: tape, knife, jelly beans, dolls, a large chart with two rows (boys/girls), draw square-sized stick figures of boys/girls on 2" squares of paper (use a size to fit the chart squares)

As children arrive, ask them if they are a boy or a girl. Give them a stick-figure picture of a boy or a girl accordingly. Then ask if their doll is a boy or girl. Give them another picture.

Explain: In our Bible lesson today we will talk about how God made boys and girls. Let's find out how many boys and how many girls we have in our class.

1. Put your picture in the column that shows if you are a boy or a girl.

2. Next put your picture in the column that shows if your doll is a boy or girl.

- If some of the children bring in stuffed animals instead, ask if it is a boy or girl.
- Let the children help you count how many boys and how many girls are in your class.
- Next COUNT how many boy dolls and how many girl dolls there are. Does it match?
- Summarize: God made BOTH boys and girls. I am glad we have BOTH in our class!
- Show clear glass container with jelly beans. These jelly beans are all different colors. But when I cut them open, they have the same stuff on the inside. Just like all of us are different on the outside, but the same inside.

HOW are we the same? *(heart, red blood, etc.)*

Older Children

Supplies Needed: none

Explain:

- When God made us, He made us to "match" on both sides of our bodies. We have an arm on one side, and we have another arm on the other side.

- Both arms are not the same, otherwise one would come out at our shoulder like normal, and the other one would have our fingers attached to our shoulder! *(Demonstrate by standing up and stretching arms out.)*

- Our bodies are "symmetrical." It is more like our arms are mirror images of each other. Now I want you to choose a friend and then we'll all practice being mirrors for each other.

"MIRROR" Each Other:

1. Allow children time to get a partner. Ask them to turn and face each other.

2. Call out a body movement. Ask the children to do that movement.
Explain: When I say "raise your hand," both of you must raise one hand on the same side of your body. Try it. Now put your hand down. Raise one knee.

3. Continue until children understand what to do as they learn to "read" each other. *(You may want to ask the children not to talk.)*

4. Let children take turns thinking of other body movements.

Learning Centers

 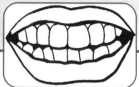  

Art Center

NOTE: This art project can be done as a large group exercise or as a center activity.

Supplies Needed: small plain paper plates or circles of various "skin tones," markers, yarn, glue sticks, and mirrors (show picture of globe with children's faces in CREATION Big Book)

Explain: Today we are going to make a picture of ourselves the way God made us.
The paper plate will be our face. Let's add the other parts of our face with the markers.
It will be fun to make the paper "face" look like you do!

Demonstrate: So if I want to make a picture of me the way God made me, and I have brown eyes, what color of eyes am I going to put on my paper plate? Brown. If you are not sure what color your eyes are, you can look in the mirror.

What color is my mouth? Should I add freckles? What about my hair? We will use yarn for hair. What color is my hair? That's the color I will use on my picture. What about you?

(Show how to cut some pieces of yarn and glue them on for hair.) Now you try.
Some children will need extra help with this to make their plate picture look like a person.

Younger Children

Supplies Needed: dolls, props for playing house

Allow children to play with the dolls and props in any way that they want as long as it is appropriate.

Dramatic play is a wonderful way for young children to practice being grown up. Role play helps them put themselves in perspective and helps prepare them for roles as adults.

Children who are hesitant may need some help getting started.
Play together: This is my baby. Where is your baby? I am going to give my baby some breakfast.

Oh dear! He just spilled his cereal. Does your baby ever do that?

I'm so glad God gave me this wonderful little baby. I wonder what he will be when he grows up. Tell me about your baby.

Play should progress easily. If there are not enough babies for each child, let a few of the children assume the role of a neighbor, a big brother, or of the dog.

Invite children to come to Circle Time to join you.

Circle Time Song

Review the "Creation Song."
Sing to the tune of "Frere Jacques" ("Are You Sleeping?").

On Day one, on Day one,
God did make, God did make
Light to shine in darkness,
Light to shine in darkness.
It was good. It was good.

On Day two, on Day two,
God did make, God did make
Lots of sky and water,
Lots of sky and water.
It was good. It was good.

On Day three, on Day three,
God did make, God did make
Many trees and flowers,
Many trees and flowers.
It was good. It was good.

On Day four, on Day four,
God did make, God did make
Sun and moon and stars,
Sun and moon and stars.
It was good. It was good.

On Day five, on Day five,
God did make, God did make
All the fish and birdies,
All the fish and birdies.
It was good. It was good.

On Day six, on Day six,
God did make, God did make
All the other animals,
All the other animals.
God made man, woman too.

*   *   *

Other songs:
"Everything Is Possible"
"God Is So Good"
"He's Got the Whole World"
"Heads and Shoulders, Knees and Toes"

Circle Time Discussion

Who made people? God did.
How did God make Adam? *(God formed Adam out of "the dust of the ground.")*

This would be like making a man out of dirt and mud, and then making him come to life. Could you and I do that?
(No. Only God can make a living person.)

Adam was made in "the image of God." Adam was a lot different from the birds and fish and other animals, wasn't he?
How was Adam special? *(He could talk with God. He could love. He could laugh. He could think big thoughts and make things in ways the animals couldn't. Adam was special!)*

God made TWO kinds of people. Do you remember what kinds? Yes, men and women. Why do you think God made a man and a woman? *(Take all responses.)*

The Bible tells us God knew Adam only had animals for his friends. God knew Adam needed someone to help him and work with him.

So God made Eve and brought her to Adam. Do you think Adam was happy to see Eve?
God wanted Adam and Eve to rule over, or be in charge of, all the plants and animals.

What a big job for two people! Then God told Adam and Eve to have children. Now what could the children do? *(Help take care of the earth and the animals. Now turn back in the Big Book and look at all the different kinds of plants and animals, fish, and birds.)*

Your mommy and daddy also have a lot of work to do. What are some of the ways you help your mommy and daddy? *(Take all responses.)* Isn't it good to know God made all of us? We're glad God made us special!

Now let's practice our Bible Memory Verse.

Practice the Memory Verse

"The Lord God formed man of the dust of the ground, and breathed into his nostrils the breath of life; and man became a living soul" (Genesis 2:7 KJV).

The Bible tells us God breathed the breath of life into Adam and he came alive.

Can people make anything come alive?
Can we breathe into our dolls and make them come to life? I don't think so, but let's try.

(Wait while children try to breathe life into dolls.)

Does it work for us? No! But it worked for God. Let's say the verse to our dolls, "God breathed the breath of life in him" (Gen. 2:7).

Did your doll hear you? Why not?
The doll is not alive. Let's try again. *(Repeat until children seem comfortable saying the verse.)*

Post-Session Learning Centers

(After Circle Time, rotate children to another Learning Center)

Closing • Back to Circle Time

At the end of the class, gather the children together for a closing circle. Have the children tell what their favorite part of the day was.
Help them review each step.

Then pray together:
Thank You, God, for making each one of us special. Thank You for giving us life. We are so glad You love us and stay close to us always. We pray in Jesus' Name. Amen.

Do you know if God made anything else? We'll see next week.

Remember to send home Parent Page

Dear Parents,

Today: we learned God gave us life. We made an art project picture of ourselves. We learned how God made us the same in some ways and also different because there is a different plan for each of us. We all used our ears and then our fingers. Ask your child to sing the Creation Song. Find out what his/her favorite part of today was.

Next Week: We will talk about the seventh day of creation, the day of rest. This is a good week for you and your child to take some "down time." A "picnic rest" on a blanket outside, or in some unusual place *(like under the table)* may be more exciting than just a plain "nap."

Read: Genesis 2:1–3 with your child. Pray for each family member to get enough rest this week.

Things to Bring Next Week: a pillow to rest on

For Parents: In our culture, rest is not something that comes naturally for adults, especially parents of young children. Jesus said, "The Sabbath was made for man" (Mark 2:27). The Sabbath day of rest is a gift to us. Keeping the Sabbath will give us more energy to tackle our week. Think of something fun and non-stressful to do on your day of rest.

Blessings to your family from our Teaching Staff

Dear Parents,

Lesson 10

Today: we learned God gave us life. We made an art project picture of ourselves. We learned how God made us the same in some ways and also different because there is a different plan for each of us. We all used our ears and then our fingers. Ask your child to sing the Creation Song. Find out what his/her favorite part of today was.

Next Week: We will talk about the seventh day of creation, the day of rest. This is a good week for you and your child to take some "down time." A "picnic rest" on a blanket outside, or in some unusual place *(like under the table)* may be more exciting than just a plain "nap."

Read: Genesis 2:1–3 with your child. Pray for each family member to get enough rest this week. **Things to Bring Next Week:** a pillow to rest on

For Parents: In our culture, rest is not something that comes naturally for adults, especially parents of young children. Jesus said, "The Sabbath was made for man" (Mark 2:27). The Sabbath day of rest is a gift to us. Keeping the Sabbath will give us more energy to tackle our week. Think of something fun and non-stressful to do on your day of rest.

Blessings to your family from our Teaching Staff

God Creates PEOPLE

"The Lord God formed man of the dust of the ground, and breathed into his nostrils the breath of life; and man became a living soul" (Genesis 2:7, 22 KJV).

God Made My Body

(Sing to the tune of
 "Hokey-Pokey")
Traditional Singing Game

You put your one foot in,
You put your one foot out,
You put your one foot in
And you shake it all about.
You do the hokey-pokey,
And you turn yourself around.
That's what it's all about.

Additional Verses:

You put your TWO feet in . . .
You put your one hand in . . .
You put your two hands in . . .
You put your head in . . .
You put your head out . . .
You put your whole self in . . .
You put your whole self out . . .
(Can vary with other parts of body: elbow, arm, etc.)

Pantomime Poem   by Helen Haidle

Stand up with the children.
Act out the motions in this poem.

Explain:
The Lord gave each of us a wonderful body
that can do many things. Now let's do
the actions of this poem together.

Blink both of your eyes;
Now shut them up tight.
Pretend you're asleep
On your pillow at night.

Pretend to wake up
When you hear the alarm. *(Ring!)*
Now open your eyes,
And stretch out your arm.

Let's all brush our teeth,
And comb out our hair.
And now let's decide
What we're going to wear.

Pretend to get dressed.
Put shoes on your feet.
Then run to the kitchen
It's breakfast! Let's eat!

First we all bow our heads,
And give thanks for our food:
"We thank You, dear Lord,
You're so great and so GOOD."
                    Amen!

God Creates a Day of Rest

"And on the seventh day God ended his work which he had made; and he rested on the seventh day from all his work which he had made. And God blessed the seventh day, and sanctified it: because that in it he had rested from all his work" (Genesis 2:2–3 KJV).

Get Ready:

☐ **PRAY** throughout the week that God will bless you and your children with understanding of the awesome power of His creation.

☐ **MAKE COPIES** of the parent take-home page.

☐ **CONTACT ASSISTANTS** to remind them that you look forward to working with them. Go over the things you would like them to do in class.

☐ **PREPARE** and set up a resting area for children to use with pillows at any time during class today. May add restful music playing quietly in the background.

☐ **GATHER** *The Creation Story for Children* (optional) plus other materials for your centers and circle time.

Welcome parents and children as they arrive. Remember to call each one by name if you can. Invite children to join one of the learning centers.

Learning Center Supplies

Physical Center
none *(optional: alarm clock, CD of peaceful music)*

Science Center
tub of warm water with plastic sea creatures and sea-shells, towels, and a plastic tablecloth

Art Center
paper plates, jumbo craft sticks, tape, and markers

Older/Younger Students
- pictures of different kinds of animals, or a large book on animals *(Include animals who sleep at night and those who sleep during the day.)*
- dolls and props for playing house, hand towel for doll blankets, blanket/sleeping bag for children

Learning Centers

(To involve children before and after Circle Time Learning)

Physical Center

Option #1

Supplies Needed: none (Optional: alarm clock for "waking up")

Explain: Today we are going to play a working and resting game.

1. Each of us will think of one thing we can do that is WORK.
2. Then we will pretend to do that "work" six times.
3. Then, instead of doing the work again, we will lie down and rest.

I'll start. One hard work job we can do is to dig a hole.
(Act out digging a hole with a shovel as you pretend to pour the dirt to the side.)

Everyone count with me while we dig 6 holes. 1, 2, 3, 4, 5, 6, rest!
On "rest," we should all lie down on the floor and close our eyes.
(Give them a minute to simulate falling asleep.)

Ding! Ding! There's the alarm! Time to get up and work again!
Who wants think of some work we can do next before we rest again?
(Continue until everyone has had a turn or as long as interest lasts.)

Physical Center

Option #2

Supplies Needed: none
Optional: CD of peaceful music

Direct children who want to rest to the area you have prepared for them.

They may take their pillows and stay to rest as long as they want.

Have one adult talk with them about rest and lead the discussion. Close with a special prayer of thanks to God for rest.

- When do you rest? Every day? In the afternoon? After lunch? After playtime?

- Where is your favorite place to rest? On a sofa, a special chair, under a table?

- What might happen if you DON'T take any rest during the day or week? *(Get grouchy, fuss or cry a lot, get sick, etc.)*

- Do you pray a special prayer when you lay down to sleep? Tell it to us.

- Let's thank God right now for REST.

Learning Centers

Science Center

Supplies Needed: tub of warm water with towels, seashells, and plastic sea creatures

Allow three or four children at a time to play in the water. Warm water play can be very soothing. Try not to interrupt their conversation or their play unless it seems to be heading in the wrong direction. Keep everything very relaxing, peaceful, and restful today.

Discuss:
Who made the water and the fish? Who made sea creatures? On what day were they made?
Does this water remind you of being in the bathtub? Do you enjoy water?
Do you think God smiled when He looked over everything He had made?
Yes, and God said it ALL was good.

God looked at all the sea creatures and birds and called them "good."

God made animals, a man and a woman and called everything "VERY GOOD!"

Doesn't that make *you* feel good?
And now it is a good time to REST.
Why is rest important for us every day?
Let's wipe off our hands and head over to the rest place with all the pillows.

Older Children

Supplies Needed: pictures of different kinds of animals, or a large book on animals

God knows it's important to rest. ALL people and animals need REST.
- Some animals rest at night. These are called diurnal animals.
- Others rest during the day. They are call nocturnal animals.

Now we will look at pictures of different animals. You tell me if you think they rest at night, like most people do, or if they rest during the daytime.

Show pictures and allow children to discuss the animals and what they do.
<u>Nocturnal animals</u> include: rats, raccoons, bats, opossums, owls, moles, mice, hamsters, and ocelots.
<u>Diurnal animals</u> include most farm animals such as horses, cows, pigs, plus other animals like dogs, giraffes, elephants, etc.

Learning Centers

Art Center

NOTE: This art project can be done as a large-group exercise or as a center activity.

Supplies Needed: paper plates, jumbo craft sticks, tape, and markers

1. Ask children to draw pictures of themselves AWAKE on one side of the plate.

2. Turn the plate over. Ask them to draw a picture of themselves ASLEEP on the other side of the plate.

3. Tape a jumbo craft stick to the bottom of the plate, forming a stick "puppet."

4. Now have children turn their plate—puppet to the appropriate action as you name different parts of the day when they rest or are awake.

   REST: after lunch, after a trip in the car, after an activity, etc.

   AWAKE: eat dinner, play in sandbox, set table, pick up toys, go to store, etc.

   (NOTE: Go over the list of activities more than once.)

Younger Children

Supplies Needed: dolls and props for playing house. Include some hand towels to use as blankets for the dolls (May also include sleeping bags or blankets for the children.)

This is an extension of the dramatic play that was started last week.
The focus this week, though, is the REST.
Watch the children as they go through their bedtime routine.

"It is time for me to put my baby to bed. What should I do first?"

Allow children to walk you through bath, story, prayer, like they do at bedtime or at nap time. Some children may not be able or willing to tell you what to do next. If you suspect this to be true, simply ask, "Can you show me?"

Invite children to come to Circle Time to join you.

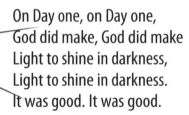

Circle Time Song

Review the first six verses of the "Creation Song."
Teach the last verse. Sing to the tune of "Frere Jacques."

On Day one, on Day one,
God did make, God did make
Light to shine in darkness,
Light to shine in darkness.
It was good. It was good.

On Day two, on Day two,
God did make, God did make
Lots of sky and water,
Lots of sky and water.
It was good. It was good.

On Day three, on Day three,
God did make, God did make
Many trees and flowers,
Many trees and flowers.
It was good. It was good.

On Day four, on Day four,
God did make, God did make
Sun and moon and stars,
Sun and moon and stars.
It was good. It was good.

On Day five, on Day five,
God did make, God did make
All the fish and birdies,
All the fish and birdies.
It was good. It was good.

On Day six, on Day six,
God did make, God did make
All the other animals,
All the other animals.
God made man, woman too.

(more slowly)
On Day seven, on Day seven,
God did rest, God did rest.
All the work was finished,
All the work was finished.
It was good, very good!

* * *

Other Songs:
"Everything Is Possible"
"He's Got the Whole World"
"Head and Shoulders"
"Jesus Loves Me"
"God Is So Good"

Circle Time Discussion

There are two major points to discuss. The first is that God finished the work of creation. The second is that God rested.

Look at the man and the woman. What are they doing? *(Relaxing, watching the animals, petting a lion, enjoying the sunset.)*

They are looking at all of the things God made. Do they see light? Do they see sky and water? Do they see land and flowers and trees?

All the things God planned to make were now all made. Everything God made was very good. So do you know what God did next? God rested.

What do you suppose God wants us to do after we work very hard? Rest!

Are we supposed to rest all day? No. But we are not supposed to work all the time either.

Who has an idea about WHY God wants us to rest sometimes? *(Take all ideas.)*

God wants us to rest because it is good for our bodies. Rest is also good for our minds.

What happens when you spend time outdoors in God's beautiful creation?

Does it make you feel good to be out in God's creation? Does it make you happy or mad? Does it put people in a good mood or bad mood? Do you feel upset or more peaceful when you are outdoors?

What are some of the things you do when you rest? *(Take all answers . . . curl up on the sofa, cover up with a blanket, get a special pillow, take off shoes, get a stuffed animal, etc.)*

Where are some places you go to see and enjoy God's beautiful creation? *(Take all answers. Taking time to rest also reminds us of how much God loves us and wants us to spend time with Him.)*

Now let's practice our Bible Memory Verse.

Practice the Memory Verse

"On the seventh day God ended his work... and he rested on the seventh day from all the work which he had made" (Genesis 2:2 KJV).

Practice this verse several times as you do lots of stretching and yawning and sleepily closing your eyes. Remind children how much God loves them and cares for them each day.

Children who are in the resting area do not have to practice out loud. If you go through it several times, and they hear it, they will probably remember it very well.

Post-Session Learning Centers

(After Circle Time, rotate children to another Learning Center)

Closing · Back to Circle Time

At the end of the class, gather the children together for a closing circle. Let the children **tell** what their favorite part of the day was. Help them **review** each step.

Then pray together:

Thank You, God, for loving us. Thank You for creating our world. Thank You for flowers, trees, and mountains. Thank You for lakes and rivers, fish and birds, and lots of animals. Thank You for making us special. And thank You for teaching us how to rest. Help us to remember we need to rest often. In Jesus' Name. Amen.

Remember to send home Parent Page

Dear Parents,

Today: We learned what it means to "rest." We played a working and resting game. We talked about what we do when we are awake and asleep. Ask your child to sing the Creation Song. Find out what his/her favorite part of today was.

Next Time: We will talk about Psalm 139 and how God formed us inside our mother's body. We will learn how God never leaves us and always knows where we are. We belong to God.

Read: Psalm 139:13–18 with your child. Pray for your teacher and thank God for giving us our lives. Praise God for the assurance that He is always with us, no matter what happens.

Bring Next Time: one or two pieces of any kind of fabric cut about 4x4" wide.

For Parents: Read Psalm 139 and meditate on it for your own encouragement. God knows all about every detail of your life today and in the future. Rejoice that God never leaves you. And God considers us to be very precious, like our children are to us . . . only much, much more!

Blessings to your family from our Teaching Staff

Dear Parents,

Lesson 11

Today: We learned what it means to "rest." We played a working and resting game. We talked about what we do when we are awake and asleep. Ask your child to sing the Creation Song. Find out what his/her favorite part of today was.

Next Time: We will talk about Psalm 139 and how God formed us inside our mother's body. We will learn how God never leaves us and always knows where we are. We belong to God.

Read: Psalm 139:13–18 with your child. Pray for your teacher and thank God for giving us our lives. Praise God for the assurance that He is always with us, no matter what happens.

Bring Next Time: one or two pieces of any kind of fabric cut about 4x4" wide.

For Parents: Read Psalm 139 and meditate on it for your own encouragement. God knows all about every detail of your life today and in the future. Rejoice that God never leaves you. And God considers us to be very precious, like our children are to us . . . only much, much more!

Blessings to your family from our Teaching Staff

God Creates a Day of Rest

"And on the seventh day God ended his work which he had made; and he rested on the seventh day... And God blessed the seventh day, and sanctified it: because that in it he had rested from all his work" (Genesis 2:2-3 KJV).

Take Time for Creativity

When we stop to rest and relax, sometimes God gives us new ideas.
There are many ways we demonstrate God's creativity in our lives.
Here are a couple of ideas to stimulate children's God–given creativity.

1. Lay out supplies of construction paper, old magazines, various stickers of animals, birds, insects, etc. Let each child **create his or her own unique collage of CREATION.** Give them time to share their pictures.

2. Encourage children to **make up a new song** no one has ever heard.
   Applaud them as they exercise the creativity God gave them.
   (NOTE: Ask for a volunteer to share. There are usually a couple of children who will spontaneously sing or chant something "new." This will encourage other children to try it themselves.)

A Resting Game:

"Guess What God Made?"

Before class, fill a fancy gift bag with a variety of fruits and vegetables: a kiwi, an orange, an apple, a banana, a carrot, a potato, a grape, broccoli, a zucchini, a pea pod, a tomato, a cucumber, a grapefruit, a lemon, etc.

1. Hold up the bag. Ask for a volunteer to put his or her hand in the bag *(without peeking)* and select ONE item. Do NOT pull it out of the sack. Ask the child to keep their hand in the bag and only gently TOUCH and FEEL with their fingers.

2. Let child try to guess what he is holding in his hand.

3. Now have the child pull out the item and see if his guess was correct.

4. Place food item on a large platter while you make a few statements about how good the item is to eat or touch or smell, etc.

5. Let children take turns repeating the above until everything in the bag is guessed.

6. Slice up some of the fruit. Insert toothpicks. Serve for a snack.

God Created ME!

"O Lord, thou hast searched me, and known me. . . thou hast covered me in my mother's womb. I will praise thee; for I am fearfully and wonderfully made" (Psalm 139:1, 13, 14 KJV).

PSALM 139
Best of all, the LORD God, Creator of heaven and earth, made YOU!

"O LORD . . .
You created the deepest parts of my being.
You put me together inside my mother's body.
. . .When you were putting me together . . .
your eyes saw my body
even before it was formed."

Psalm 139:13, 15–16

Welcome parents and children as they arrive. Remember to call each one by name. Invite children to join one of the learning centers.

Get Ready:

☐ **PRAY** throughout the week that God will bless you and your children with understanding of the awesome power of His creation.

☐ **MAKE COPIES** of the parent take-home page.

☐ **CONTACT ASSISTANTS** to remind them that you look forward to working with them. Go over the things you would like them to do in class.

☐ **PREPARE** and precut a variety of construction paper strips about 1" wide for older children to use for weaving.

☐ **GATHER** *The Creation Story for Children* (optional) plus other materials for your centers and circle time.

Learning Center Supplies

Physical Center
#1 – none
#2 – animal crackers

Science Center
a variety of fabric pieces (heavier threads to pull out) magnifying glasses, and tweezers

Art Center
a variety of pieces of fabric, construction paper, markers and glue, blackboard, chalk

Older/Younger Students
• strips of construction paper, whole pieces of construction paper, tape
• none

Learning Centers

(To involve children before and after Circle Time Learning)

Physical Center

Option #1

Supplies Needed: none

Let's play "Hide and Seek!"

NOTE: This reinforces the fact that no matter where we go, God knows where we are, and God is there with us. *(You may have to set aside a portion of the room for hide and seek so children working at the other centers aren't disturbed.)*

Explain:

1. I am going to count to 15 while you find a place to hide.

2. When I finish counting, I will come and try to find each one of you.

3. Hold still. Be very quiet where you are hiding. Try not to let me see you.

4. The last person found can be the "finder" for our next game.

Summarize: If I were God, would I have to look for you? No. God already knows where each person is hiding. Remember, even when no one else can see you, God can.

And God can see clearly in the dark. Nothing is ever hidden from God. But now let's have some fun as we try to hide from each other one more time! *(Continue as long as there is time and interest.)*

Physical Center

Option #2

Supplies Needed: animal crackers

Explain: How God made us is amazing and wonderful. God gave each of us a great imagination. We can pretend to be a lot of things. Let's use our imaginations to play "Animal Charades" and pretend to be an animal.

1. One person will be it.

2. That person will draw one animal cracker out of the box. Then he will try to act like that animal.

3. The other children will try to guess what that animal is.

4. If the person who is it does a really good job, and the other children guess what he is, he gets to eat the cracker!

5. Now help them understand what to do: **"Watch me — I'll go first!"**

NOTE: Demonstrate what you want the children to do. When they guess what animal you are, show great enjoyment as you eat the cracker. You will have many volunteers to go next!

Learning Centers

Science Center

Supplies Needed: a variety of fabric pieces children (or teachers) brought from home, magnifying glasses, and tweezers

Explain:
The Bible tells us God put each of us together when we were growing inside our mothers. Do you think it took a lot of work to make our whole body and every little eyelash and fingernail?

Let's try taking little threads off our fabric pieces.

Look under the magnifying glass and use the tweezers to pull five–ten threads out of the fabric.

See how all the threads have been woven together to make the fabric. And this fabric is only a very simple flat piece. It wasn't hard to make.

Wouldn't it take a whole lot more work to put a <u>whole person</u> together? Oh, YES!

Does God care how we turn out?
Does God care what happens to us each day?
Does God care how we act?
Yes! God cares about every detail of our lives. God cares about everything we say and do, even about our attitudes.

(NOTE: Ask children to save the rest of their fabric for use in the art center.)

Older Children

Supplies Needed: 1–2" wide strips of construction paper, whole pieces of construction paper, plus some tape

1. Show the children how to tape five-six strips of paper onto a whole piece of construction paper. All the strips should lie horizontally side-by-side.
2. Next use different colored strips to demonstrate weaving over and under the first set.
3. Explain how to alternate the strips when you begin so the woven texture remains.

Explain: Weaving is one way that people make fabrics or rugs. It takes a lot of concentration and you have to practice to get it right. When you get good at it you can make your weaving look different by adding different colors and making different designs.

Imagine how much God thought about us before ever making us. The Bible says God "knit" us together. "Knitting" is even harder than weaving! God has given us each such an amazing body. Can you name some of the amazing things your body can do?
Let's always thank God for making our wonderful bodies.

Learning Centers

Art Center

My Self-Portrait

Supplies Needed: pieces of fabric children brought from home, construction paper, markers and glue, blackboard, and chalk

Give each child a piece of construction paper and explain:

Today we are going to use our fabric to show how different we can be.

1. Glue your piece of fabric on the construction paper.

2. Use the fabric piece as your body. Draw your head and the rest of yourself.

   (Demonstrate by drawing a square on the blackboard for the piece of fabric.)
   Each of us has a head. *(Draw a circle at the top edge of the square.)*
   We each have a nose *(Draw a nose in the circle.)* **and two eyes.**
   (Draw in two more circles for eyes, with an iris and pupil and eyelashes.)

3. See how we will all look different and special, just the way God planned!
   "How [God] made me is amazing and wonderful." Now you try to make yourself.

When the children finish, display their pictures on a bulletin board or window ledge. Allow them to notice things that are the SAME and things that are DIFFERENT about each picture.

Younger Children

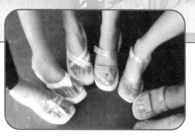 

Supplies Needed: nothing

1. Invite children to sit down with you.

2. Explain: How God made us is amazing and wonderful. God made our bodies to do lots of interesting things! Let's see how many things our bodies can do. I can pat my head. *(Demonstrate.)* Can you pat your head? *(Wait and help, if needed.)*

3. Continue: I can stick out my tongue. Can you stick out your tongue?

4. Expand discussion: What else can our bodies do? *(Wink eye, chew food, etc.)*

5. Continue to demonstrate various action-motions as long as interest and time last. Let children take turns doing things with the wonderful body God gave them. *(Raise arms, wave, crawl, lift leg, bend knee, wiggle toes, bend elbow, clap in rhythm, tickle neighbor, etc.)*

Invite children to come to Circle Time to join you.

Circle Time Song

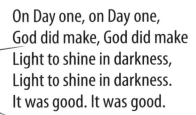

Review the verses of the "Creation Song." Sing to the tune of "Frere Jacques."

On Day one, on Day one,
God did make, God did make
Light to shine in darkness,
Light to shine in darkness.
It was good. It was good.

On Day two, on Day two,
God did make, God did make
Lots of sky and water,
Lots of sky and water.
It was good. It was good.

On Day three, on Day three,
God did make, God did make
Many trees and flowers,
Many trees and flowers.
It was good. It was good.

On Day four, on Day four,
God did make, God did make
Sun and moon and stars,
Sun and moon and stars.
It was good. It was good.

On Day five, on Day five,
God did make, God did make
All the fish and birdies,
All the fish and birdies.
It was good. It was good.

On Day six, on Day six,
God did make, God did make
All the other animals,
All the other animals.
God made man, woman too.

(more slowly)
On Day seven, on Day seven,
God did rest, God did rest.
All the work was finished,
All the work was finished.
It was good, very good!

*   *   *

Other songs:
"Head and Shoulders"
"Jesus Loves the Little Children"
"Jesus Loves Me"
"God Is So Good"
"God Made Me"

Circle Time Discussion

Read Psalm 139:13–16

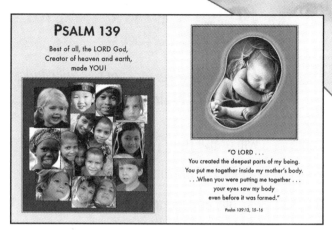

Discuss:
God is telling us two very important things in this part of the Bible.

1. When we were made, God made us on purpose. God has a plan for you. God made us amazing and wonderful, just the way God wanted us to be.

Did God make all of us the same? Yes.
In what ways are we the same? We all have a head with two eyes, two ears, a nose, and a mouth. We have a heart, etc.

But do we all look the same? *(No.)*
Each of us, even twins, look different, think differently, and make things in our own way, just the way God planned.

2. The second thing is that God, who is always with us, knows where we are. God also knows what we are doing and what we are thinking all the time.

So, if we are at home in our rooms, does God know where we are? If we are on vacation, does God know where we are?

If we get lost in the store, does God know where we are? Yes! God is always WITH us and God loves us and KNOWS all about us.

So, if you ever get lost in a store, you don't have to be afraid. You can pray, "God, please help me find my parents."
Then go to a person working at the cash register and tell him you need to find your parents.

(Note: Be sure to tell the children to go to someone who works at the cash register and not just to any adult in the store.)

God will always help you because God knows where YOU are and also where your parents are. God can even see you in the dark.

Have you ever been lost from your parents, or tried to hide from them? Did God help your parents find you? How? *(Allow children time to tell.)*

Remember: God has been with you ever since your life started growing inside your mother. God loves you!
And God will never ever leave you.
Isn't that amazing and wonderful?

Now let's practice our Bible Memory Verse.

Practice the Memory Verse

"I will praise thee; for I am fearfully and wonderfully made" (Psalm 139:14 KJV).

I will praise thee *(Point to heaven)*

for I am *(Point to self)*

fearfully and wonderfully made
(Flat hands on side of cheeks or hug self)

Psalm 139:14

- Repeat memory verse several times until children are comfortable saying it.

- Repeat verse again, but omit one line at a time *(beginning with the last line)*.

- Let the children "fill in the blank" until they can say it easily.

Post-Session Learning Centers

(After Circle Time, rotate children to another Learning Center)

Closing • Back to Circle Time

At the end of the class, gather the children together for a closing circle.
Have the children **tell** what their favorite part of the day was.
Help them **review** what they learned.

Then pray together:

Thank You, God, for always being with us every day and night.

Thank You for making us special, just the way You planned.

We're glad we belong to YOU. Thank You for loving us. Amen.

Remember to send home Parent Page

Dear Parents,

Today: we learned about Psalm 139 and how God put us together. We practiced doing amazing things with our bodies. We played hide-and-seek and remembered how God always sees us and never leaves us. God knows everything about us, even our thoughts.

Next Time: We will have a Creation CELEBRATION party with balloons, games, and special snacks as we review God's creation of the world.

Read: Psalm 139:1–12 with your child. Give thanks each day for the gift of our life.

Bring Next Time: Ask your child to bring in one of the things he/she likes about the world that God made. It can be a seashell, a picture of a pet, a stuffed animal, a flower, or some wonderful, edible plant. For our time of celebration, children can also come dressed as their favorite animal or person.

For Parents: Take time to re-read and meditate on Psalm 139. What does this Psalm mean for your life today? Let God's Word give you new perspective on who YOU are and who HE is.

Blessings to your family from our Teaching Staff

copy and distribute

Dear Parents,

Lesson
12

Today: we learned about Psalm 139 and how God put us together. We practiced doing amazing things with our bodies. We played hide-and-seek and remembered how God always sees us and never leaves us. God knows everything about us, even our thoughts.

Next Time: We will have a Creation CELEBRATION party with balloons, games, and special snacks as we review God's creation of the world.

Read: Psalm 139:1–12 with your child. Give thanks each day for the gift of our life.

Bring Next Time: Ask your child to bring in one of the things he/she likes about the world that God made. It can be a seashell, a picture of a pet, a stuffed animal, a flower, or some wonderful, edible plant. For our time of celebration, children can also come dressed as their favorite animal or person.

For Parents: Take time to re-read and meditate on Psalm 139. What does this Psalm mean for your life today? Let God's Word give you new perspective on who YOU are and who HE is.

Blessings to your family from our Teaching Staff

God Created ME

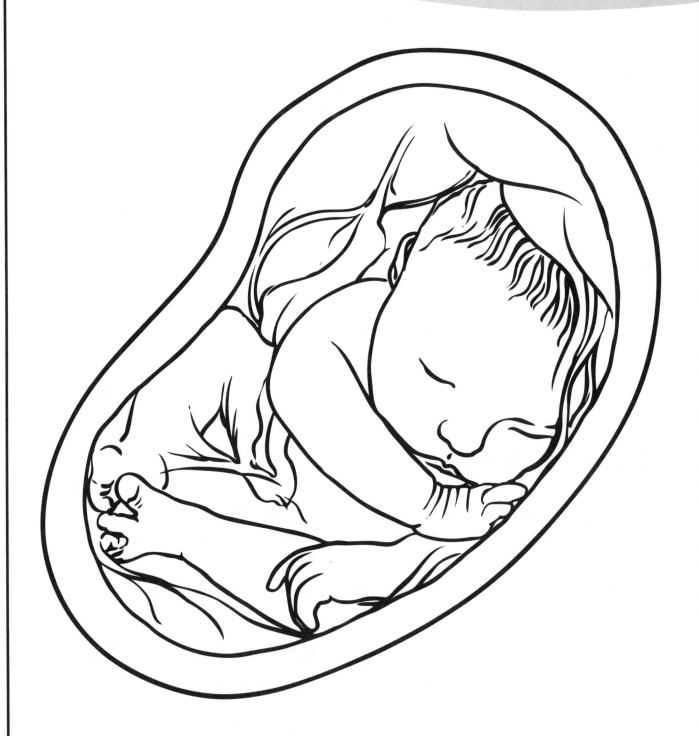

"O Lord, thou hast searched me, and known me... thou hast covered me in my mother's womb. I will praise thee; for I am fearfully and wonderfully made"
(Psalm 139:1, 13, 14 KJV).

God Made Me! — *Read Psalm 139:13–18*

Materials Needed: magnifying glasses, ink pads, paper, pencils and/or markers

Children are fascinated with details about their own bodies.
Here are some ideas to help them see themselves as unique creations of God:

1. Bring several MAGNIFYING GLASSES to class. Have children look closely at their finger nails, skin, knuckles, palm of hand, etc.

2. Show children where to locate their HEART PULSE on their left inner wrist and on the side of left inner jaw/neck.

3. Help children find their BONES — Look for all the small bones in fingers, hands, jaw, ankle, nose, etc. Then find the biggest bones in arms and legs.

4. ACTIVITY: Using an INK PAD, make an print of each child's index finger on a piece of white paper. Point out the different circular patterns found on the "pad" of each finger.

   • Remind children that everyone in the world has different fingerprints.
   • Give children time to draw a picture, using their fingerprint.
   • WRITE on each paper: *"God made me very special!"*

Guess Who I Am

I'm God's special creature — the dearest and BEST;
Unique and quite diff'rent from all of the rest.
It takes me a whole year to learn how to walk;
God 'specially designed me to smile, sing, and talk!
My design was created by God up above;
I am full of God's life: I can laugh, hug, and LOVE!
God made me to be a . . . BABY!

Creation MOBILE

The Lord is My Creator

Supplies Needed: colored pencils, scissors, tape or glue, assorted yard or ribbon, a coat hanger for each child

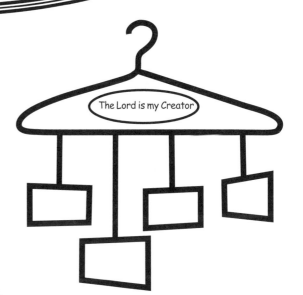

1. Photocopy this page and opposite page.

2. Color the figures in the boxes. Color oval sign.

3. Cut out the rectangle figures on the SOLID lines.

4. Fold the images in the rectangles with DOTTED lines.

5. Tape or glue 6" of ribbon in the fold of the double images. Tape the folded images back to back.

6. Use yarn or ribbon to attach images to a coat hanger at different lengths.

7. Hang the oval sign "The Lord is My Creator" in the middle of the hanger as seen on the illustration above.

Team up with a partner and share your mobile.

Tell WHICH parts of Creation are pictured on your mobile.

CREATION CELEBRATION!

*"The earth belongs to the Lord.
And so does everything in it"*
(Psalms 24:1 NIrV).

Get Ready:

☐ **PRAY** throughout the week that God will bless you and your children with understanding of the awesome power of His creation.

☐ **MAKE COPIES** of the parent take-home page.

☐ **CONTACT ASSISTANTS** Go over the things you would like them to do in class.

☐ **PREPARE:** from magazines and books, cut out pictures of animals, fish, and birds. Mount on cardstock or heavy paper.

- Label 3 baskets with a picture of a fish or a bird or a mammal.
- Write the numbers one-seven on pieces of construction paper. Children need to be able to see the papers from several feet away.
- Cut out a large blue circle for each child, one per piece of construction paper.

☐ **GATHER** *The Creation Story for Children* (optional) plus other materials for your centers and circle time.

Welcome parents and children as they arrive. Remember to call each one by name. Invite children to join one of the learning centers

Learning Center Supplies

Physical Center
#1 – box of crackers, chairs to move around
#2 – animal crackers

Science Center
precut pictures of fish, animals, and birds on stiff paper, plus three baskets labeled: fins, feathers, and fur

Art Center
a blue circle for each child, animal crackers, markers, and glue sticks

Older/Younger Students
- One picture each of animals God made, tape
- party hats and supplies, a bowl of orange sections or other fruit of your choice, sliced star fruit, goldfish crackers, and animal crackers

Learning Centers

(To involve children before and after Circle Time Learning)

Physical Center

Option #1

Supplies Needed: box of crackers, set up chairs around which the "worms" will move

Today we will play "Squirmin' Herman." Squirmin' Herman is a worm. We are going to make him out of the friends in our class! Who wants to be the head?

(Choose a child who is paying attention. Hold child's hand. Ask the other children to line up next to him/her and hold hands all together.)

Now we are going to pretend we are a big, giant worm who wants to get some "food" *(crackers)* on the other side of the room.

We need to get over to the other side of the room, but we can't go in a straight line. We have to wiggle and squirm!

- Let the lead child weave back and forth across the room with other children, holding hands and following behind him. If the lead child is reluctant, you can demonstrate. Let children take turns as the "worm."

- If time allows, have all the children lie down on the floor and pretend to be individual "Squirmin' Hermans." Let them wiggle and giggle across the floor to get their "food" on the other side of the room.

Physical Center

Option #2

Supplies Needed: animal crackers

We are going to play ANIMAL CHARADES.

1. One person will be it. That person will draw one animal cracker out of the box and then try to act like that animal.

2. Then other children will try to guess what that animal is.

3. If the person who is it does a good job, and the other children guess what he is, he gets to eat the cracker!

Let's get started playing. I'll go first!

Select an animal cracker and demonstrate what you want the children to do. Have fun acting out the animal you picked.

When the children guess what animal you are, be sure to show great enjoyment as you eat your cracker.

You will have many volunteers to go next!

Learning Centers

Science Center

Supplies Needed: precut pictures of fish, animals, and birds glued or taped on stiff paper; three baskets labeled, Fins, Feathers, or Fur. Line up baskets on floor. Mark floor with a long piece of masking tape about two feet away from the row of baskets.

Today we will play "Fins, Feathers, Fur!"

I will give each of you five pictures of various creatures. You will stand behind the line and toss each picture in the right basket.

If your picture shows a fish, you will throw it in the basket marked "Fins."

If your picture shows a bear, where will you toss the picture? (*Fur basket*)

If your picture shows a turkey, where will it go? (*Feathers basket*)

Now let's try playing Fins, Feathers, Fur.

1. Give the first child three pictures to toss.

2. When each child is finished, have him/her collect the pictures and return them to you.

3. Put pictures on the bottom of your stack. Choose three new pictures for next child.

4. When ALL pictures have been tossed, shuffle those pictures in with others. Play as long as time and interest allow.

Older Children

Supplies Needed: Pictures of animals God made (one for each child), tape

Turn the pictures upside down and mix them up. Choose one for each child, but do not let them see it. Tape the picture to their backs, then EXPLAIN:

- Each of you has the picture of an animal or a bird or a fish pinned on your back.

- Now you must guess what it is.

- You can ask other children questions to help you figure out what is on your back.

For example, if you ask, "Can I fly?" and the answer is "Yes," you will know you are some kind of bird.

- If you ask, "Can I swim?" and the answer is "Yes," you might be a fish OR you might be a seal or a frog. So you have to keep asking questions until you guess right.

- Once you guess your animal correctly, you can sit down. You can still answer questions for the other children.

Now let's have fun as you try to guess your animal. Ready? Set? Go!

Learning Centers

Art Center

NOTE: This can be done as a large group exercise or as a center activity.

Supplies Needed: blue circles, animal crackers, markers, and glue sticks (maybe magazines)
Give each child a blue circle, some markers, and a handful of animal crackers.

Explain:

1. The blue circle is the earth.

2. Decide what you want to put on the earth. Draw it with your markers.

3. You can draw lakes and rivers and trees on the earth.

4. You can draw people on the earth and their houses.

5. You can also glue animals *(animal crackers)* on the earth.

6. When you are done, can you tell us to whom all these things belong?

    Yes! "The earth belongs to the Lord. And so does everything in it" (Psalm 24:1).

Alternative: *Allow children to cut the above items out of* **magazines.**
Glue cut items on the blue circles instead of drawing the items with markers.

Younger Children

Supplies Needed: party hats and supplies, a bowl of orange sections (or other fruit of your choice), sliced star fruit, goldfish crackers, and animal crackers
Explain: We are going to have a Creation Celebration! We will celebrate and thank God for all the things He made, AND we will do it in the order God made them.

First   –   Let's turn on LIGHTS *(ask a child to do this for the group).*
Second   –   Let's pour the WATER.
Third   –   Let's take turns dishing up FRUIT onto our plates.
Fourth   –   Add some STAR–fruit to your plate if you want to try it.
Fifth   –   Let's put some GoldFISH crackers on our plates.
Sixth   –   Now we can add some ANIMAL crackers on our plates.
Seventh –   Let's sit down to eat and let's pray together.
Thank You, God, for giving us a big, wonderful world to enjoy.

**Invite children to come to
Circle Time to join you.**

Circle Time Song

Today is the last day to sing our "Creation Song."
Who knows it? Sing it while I turn the pages of our book.
Sing to the tune of "Frere Jacques" *("Are You Sleeping?")*.

On Day one, on Day one,
God did make, God did make
Light to shine in darkness,
Light to shine in darkness.
It was good. It was good.

On Day two, on Day two,
God did make, God did make
Lots of sky and water,
Lots of sky and water.
It was good. It was good.

On Day three, on Day three,
God did make, God did make
Many trees and flowers,
Many trees and flowers.
It was good. It was good.

On Day four, on Day four,
God did make, God did make
Sun and moon and stars,
Sun and moon and stars.
It was good. It was good.
On Day five, on Day five,

God did make, God did make
All the fish and birdies,
All the fish and birdies.
It was good. It was good.

On Day six, on Day six,
God did make, God did make
All the other animals,
All the other animals.
God made man, woman too.

(more slowly)
On Day seven, on Day seven,
God did rest, God did rest.
All the work was finished,
All the work was finished.
It was good, very good!

*   *   *

Other songs:
"Head and Shoulders, Knees"
"Jesus Loves the Little Children"
"Jesus Loves Me"
"God Is So Good"
"God Made Me"

Circle Time Discussion

Ahead of time, tape seven pieces of construction paper *(with numbers one - seven printed on them)* on a wall or edge of a bulletin board.

God made each of us very special. We can trust God loves us very much. God knows all about us and will never leave us.

God made many wonderful rocks and birds and bugs and fish and animals.

Can any of us make things like God made just by saying the words? No.

God helps us do wonderful things, but we are not as great and wonderful as God, our loving Creator!

Did you bring to class one of your very favorite things God made? Who wants to share their favorite thing God made?

Go around the room and give each child an opportunity to show and tell about one of their favorite things God made.
(NOTE: If they didn't bring something to "show," they can just "tell.")

Do you remember on which day your favorite thing was made?

Once the correct day is identified, have the child go and stand in the line with that particular number in the front. When everyone has taken a turn, count the children in each line to see which day is their favorite day of Creation.

Now let's sit down in a circle so we can look at each other. I'm going to get in the middle of the circle. I'm going to walk around the circle and talk to all of you.

Each of you belong to the Lord. I'm glad God made every one of you very unique and special. Even your fingerprints are special. Now I'm going to tell you one thing I really like about YOU.

(Give each child an enthusiastic compliment about themselves. [i.e. "Julie, your smile cheers everyone up. Drew, you have a great imagination . . . creativity, kindness, cooperation," etc.])

YES, God made each of you very special.

Now let's practice our Bible Memory Verse.

Practice the Memory Verse

"The earth is the Lord's, and the fullness thereof; the world, and they that dwell therein" (Psalm 24:1 KJV).

"The earth belongs to the Lord. And so does every-thing in it" (Paraphrase).

- Have the children stand in a circle to represent the earth.

- Then have them recite the verse. As they say "the fullness thereof:" (or "everything in it") have them jump into the middle of the circle.

- Repeat several times.

Discuss:

Do the fish belong to the Lord?
Do the lions belong to the Lord?
Does every ostrich belong to the Lord?
Do all the stars belong to the Lord?
Does the sun and moon belong to God?

How about you and me?
Do WE belong to the Lord?
Yes! Each one of us belongs to the Lord.

Recite the verse a few more times until the children seem to know it without your help.

Post-Session Learning Centers

(After Circle Time, rotate children to another Learning Center)

Closing • Back to Circle Time

At the end of the class, gather the children together for a closing circle. Have the children tell what their favorite part of the day was. Help them review each step.

Then pray together:
Thank You, God, for making so many wonderful things in the world. Thank You for making each one of us and for making our families. We're glad we all belong to You as part of Your family! In Jesus' name. Amen.

God wants us all to remember we were made in a very special way. God wants us to know He is always with us to help us and take care of us, even during hard times. God will never stop loving us. We belong to Him. Let's say together:
"I belong to God!" *(Repeat it with them.)*

Remember to send home Parent Page

Dear Parents,

Today: we celebrated ALL of God's creation. We played animal charades and guessing games, then we did an art project of the world and things God created. Ask your child to sing the Creation Song to you. Let your child tell you what he/she liked best about today.

Read: Continue to read God's Word with your child. Pray with your child each day. As you draw close to God together, you'll experience God at work in your lives.

For Parents: Did you know that recent research shows that many of the childhood troubles children struggle with today are directly related to their lack of exposure to nature?
God gave man charge over all the plants and animals. God also uses creation itself to help take care of us! There is something very satisfying about being outside, enjoying God's world.

New research reveals that incidents of stress, depression, obesity, even ADHD have been found to improve with the amount of time children are allowed to explore in God's creation. As an adult, you may have noticed how soothing it is to your spirit as well! Why not decide this week to be outside with your child on a regular basis? You'll both be glad you did!

Blessings to your family from our Teaching Staff

Dear Parents,

Lesson 13

Today: we celebrated ALL of God's creation. We played animal charades and guessing games, then we did an art project of the world and things God created. Ask your child to sing the Creation Song to you. Let your child tell you what he/she liked best about today.

Read: Continue to read God's Word with your child. Pray with your child each day. As you draw close to God together, you'll experience God at work in your lives.

For Parents: Did you know that recent research shows that many of the childhood troubles children struggle with today are directly related to their lack of exposure to nature?
God gave man charge over all the plants and animals. God also uses creation itself to help take care of us! There is something very satisfying about being outside, enjoying God's world.

New research reveals that incidents of stress, depression, obesity, even ADHD have been found to improve with the amount of time children are allowed to explore in God's creation. As an adult, you may have noticed how soothing it is to your spirit as well! Why not decide this week to be outside with your child on a regular basis? You'll both be glad you did!

Blessings to your family from our Teaching Staff

Celebrate Creation

**"The earth is the Lord's, and the fullness thereof,
the world, and they that dwell therein"** (Psalms 24:1 KJV).

Ideas for Learning Centers

Supplies Needed: Leftovers from various art projects and favorite activities during this unit, such as sensory tubs with water, dirt, and/or cornstarch with water, dolls, and stuffed animals.

This final class in our CREATION series is a good time to remind the children of all of the beautiful and wonderful things God made for us to enjoy.

(It is also a good way to use up any leftover art materials.)

Show the children the centers you have provided.

Remind children of God's gifts of creation which are represented in each center.

Make this a festive celebration. Hand out balloons. Perhaps take the children's photos. Prepare special snacks that display many of the delicious fruits God made.

Of course you will not be able to set out EVERYTHING you have done in this unit; but as a true celebration, you could repeat some things from different parts of the unit, especially activities the children enjoyed the most.

For example, you could play a few of the games.

Or you may set up:

- a water table
- a cut and paste table that includes eathers and tissue paper
- dramatic play with dolls and stuffed animals.

Help the children enjoy all the gifts God made, and give thanks for His goodness and love!

Various Creatures

GUESS WHO I AM

We're small, fuzzy insects, who work long and hard.

We pollinate flowers that grow in your yard.

We make something golden — so sticky and sweet.

Toast always tastes better when you add our treat.

If you hear us buzzing in flowers or trees,

Stand back, please! Just watch us . . . don't poke us or tease!

God made us to be . . . HONEYBEES!

GUESS WHO I AM

We have six black legs, but we're not pesky ants.

We eat bugs that ruin your garden and plants.

Two spots have been painted on our small red backs.

They look like big "eyes," and they're oval and black.

All over your garden, we crawl and we roam.

But sooner or later, we'll "fly away home."

God made us to be . . . LADY BUGS!

GUESS WHO I AM

I hide in the winter, then crawl out in Spring,

And head for your garden — I eat everything!

I'm a small, sturdy home on my back.

I leave lots of slime from my wandering track.

I travel quite slowly with only one foot.

My trail tells the tale, 'cause I never stay put!

God made me to be a . . . SNAIL!

Various Creatures

GUESS WHO I AM

I dance as I float, like a swirling ballet;

My tentacles dangle; they swing and they sway.

I'm actually dangerous to all living things;

Please don't ever touch me — you'll find out I sting!

Although I look lovely, I'll try not to boast.

I'm named after something you spread on your toast.

God made me to be a . . . JELLYFISH

GUESS WHO I AM

Do you want a friend who is loyal and true?

I'll lick on your face . . . and I'll chew on your shoe.

Let's play! Won't you throw me a stick or a ball?

Then watch! I'll come running whenever you call.

My tail wags and wiggles to show my delight.

I'll stick close beside you all day and each day.

God made me to be a . . . DOG!

GUESS WHO I AM

I tip over garbage cans. Oh, what a mess!

Folks think I look funny. I like how I dress.

With stripes down my tail and a mask on my eyes,

It gives the impression I wear a disguise.

I search for my food as I wander at night.

I might find your garbage and give you a fright!

God made me to be a . . . RACOON!

The Creation Story for Children

Enjoy a beautifully illustrated tour of the Creation week by David and Helen Haidle. From the first day when light was created to the final day of rest, the Haidles have designed a delightful book for young people to experience the wonders of our Creator's hands.

With richly-colored illustrations and easy to read text, the Creation story is shared in a visual treat for any reader!

Perfect as part of your education program or as a treasured gift, *The Creation Story for Children* also will be an incredible addition to your school, church, or home library. It is a book that children will enjoy over and over again!

ISBN-13: 978-0-89051-565-5
32 pages • 10 x 9

Master Books®
A Division of New Leaf Publishing Group
www.masterbooks.com

LEVELS K-6
MATH LESSONS FOR A LIVING EDUCATION
A CHARLOTTE MASON FLAVOR TO MATH FOR TODAY'S STUDENT

Level K, Kindergarten
978-1-68344-176-2

Level 1, Grade 1
978-0-89051-923-3

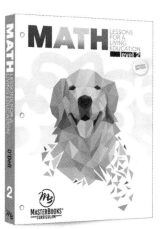

Level 2, Grade 2
978-0-89051-924-0

Level 3, Grade 3
978-0-89051-925-7

Level 4, Grade 4
978-0-89051-926-4

Level 5, Grade 5
978-0-89051-927-1

ATTRACTIVE FULL-COLOR LESSONS

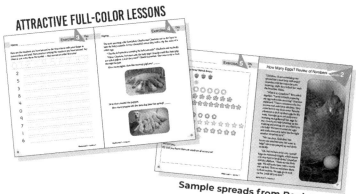

Sample spreads from Book 1

Level 6, Grade 6
978-1-68344-024-6

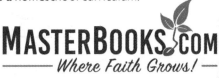